Preface

The communication problem is largely one of coping with the
quantities of information available. This can be done only through
selection, and selection is the justification of this anthology. The
material gathered here is not especially recondite in itself, but it
comes from yearbooks, newspapers, research reports, journals,
White Papers, all manner of publications. The student of Communications has normally neither the library resources, nor the
time and knowledge necessary for a proper investigation of the
field. Space and time are against him. So this source-book
presents, between one set of covers, a selection of material not
otherwise readily available. Convenience and relevance are its
aims. I have not assumed any specialist or technical knowledge
for a reading of these documents. They can be read, and discussed, by any intelligent sixth-former or College student. They
may also be of considerable interest to members of the general
public, for whom, self-evidently, the issues of modern communications are vitally important. I have, however, supplied in the
introductions to each section a minimal amount of background
commentary, together with a focusing of some of the major issues.
This should be especially helpful when this anthology is used by
seminar groups. The documents reproduced here are nevertheless
well capable of speaking for themselves.

R.B.

Contents

INTRODUCTION

SECTION III The Film

Acknowledgements

The Publishers' thanks are due to the following for permission to use copyright material:

The Times, London for 'Has television created a "reality" of its own?' by Julian Critchley; The Press Council for 'The Six Pillars of Press Council Success' by Lord Devlin from *The Annual Report of the Press Council, The Press and the People*, 13/e; Oxford University Press for an extract from *Television and the Child* by Hilde T. Himmelweit, A. N. Oppenheim and Pamela Vance (published for the Nuffield Foundation); HMSO for extracts from the *Report of the Committee on Broadcasting 1960, Cmnd. 1753*; Penguin Books Ltd for an extract from *The Contemporary Cinema* by Penelope Houston; The Independent Television Authority for 'Violence in Programmes: ITV Code' from *ITA: Annual Report, 1964–65* and an extract from *ITV 1970: A Guide to Independent Television*; Brandeis University, Waltham, Mass. for 'Television and the Kennedy Assassination' by Ruth Leeds Love; Harper & Row, Publishers Inc. and Curtis Brown Ltd for an extract from *Madison Avenue, U.S.A.* by Martin Mayer; the University of California Press for 'The Surfaces of Reality' from *Film Quarterly*, XVIII, i (1964) by permission of the Regents; and A. D. Peters & Co. for an extract from *The Advertising Man* by Jeremy Tunstall.

INTRODUCTION

I have collected here readings from a variety of fields, with the aim of throwing light on the workings of the mass media. Given the immense range of material available, such a collection must be highly selective. The main emphasis of this book is on Britain today. I have, however, devoted some space to the American experience, which offers numerous important parallels. There are various modes of communication (such as language or mime) that can be projected through the mass media, but it is clearly necessary to restrict our study to the media themselves: Press, radio, television and film. Advertising, which exploits all of these media, demanded coverage as a major purposive activity in mass communications. Reluctantly, I have had to exclude political communication; that is a book in itself.

The emphasis of the contents is on the factual; the hard statistics of newspaper circulation, the techniques by which TV audiences are counted, the numbers of radio sets among the population. These facts are verifiable, and provide a check to whatever theories of communication are currently fashionable. Much of what is written today about the mass media is opinion only. That has its place, and there is always room for informed argument and comment; but one soon tires of uninterrupted

1

theorizing. My aim has been to provide, wherever possible, a secure foundation on which readers can base their own understanding of the media.

It is essential to have the facts, to keep abreast of developments in the media. But they are constantly changing. Consequently, the introduction to each section—Press, broadcasting, film—is intended not as a definitive guide, but as a focusing of some major issues that each medium presents. I think it more useful to suggest a perspective on a rapidly-changing field, rather than provide heavily-documented introductions that will themselves become speedily obsolescent. I wish to point to certain basic issues, or principles, to which the reader can relate his own exploration of the mass media. These issues will remain relevant long after this book has gone to press.

The readings brought together here are only a selection, but they are wide-ranging. I have made no attempt at maintaining a balance of media coverage; all media are not equal. The Press, though its role has diminished, still warrants close study as a medium of entertainment, opinion formation, and straightforward dissemination of information. In this respect it is quite safe against the rise of the audio-visual media; one has only to consider the sheer bulk of information in, say, the Sunday Times, *or the* New York Times, *to appreciate that there can be no true competitor. The Press, furthermore, serves as well as any other medium to initiate a study of advertising and image-making. Next comes broadcasting, and I make no apology for the large number of documents reproduced here. Most people, I suppose, would agree that TV and radio are the most important media in the world today. Very broadly, radio is the most important medium in the underdeveloped countries (because it is inexpensive, and evades the problems of illiteracy), and TV in the developed countries. TV is quantitatively the dominant mass medium in Britain. It reaches the great majority of homes, on average for four hours each day. The exact nature of its impact is problematical, but the readings in this section provide data and suggest principles or hypotheses. The rise of TV has necessarily meant a diminution of the film's importance, but a study of the contemporary film audience, and the technique of the avant-garde film directors, has much to offer the student of*

2

communications. The film, in fact, serves to remind us of the growing phenomenon of media transference. That is to say, techniques and approaches developed in a certain medium are taken up and assimilated by another medium. This is especially marked in the shifting distinctions between TV documentary, TV drama-documentary, and the film; of late years there has been not only a movement of ideas, but of people. (Several leading TV producers have left TV to make their own films, for instance.) But in all areas there is a tendency towards cross-fertilization. Newspapers have developed the 'feature', originally a radio speciality. And straight reportage of the other media is a confirmed fact. Mr Heath has called attention to a newspaper printing on its front page the full text of a TV interview. One could equally point to a long-standing item on BBC morning radio, 'What the papers say'. Generally, the media are inter-active, and on occasion must be surveyed as a whole. It is quite normal, for instance, for a major advertising campaign to make use of several media: a theme may be broached in a colour supplement, massively elaborated in a series of TV commercials, and then fixed in the public's mind via the hoardings. It is not possible, within the limits of this anthology, to provide coverage for media transference; but it remains generally true that the media are conscious of each other today to an unprecedented degree. This should be borne in mind throughout this book, which naturally stresses the separate problems of different media. And it is true that the direction of media research in the University Centres of Communication is to make distinctions between the media, and their relative suitability for different methods of instruction. Especially of late years, the affective characteristics of each medium have become the dominant concern of the re-searchers. But the last word in this general introduction must be a warning against regarding any medium as an isolated and autonomous field.

SECTION I The Press and Advertising

The most important unit of the Press is the newspaper. It cannot achieve the instant coverage of contemporary events that broadcasting can, but its strength—extensive verbal amplification of the news—is unchallengeable. Arguably, the prime function of a newspaper is to supply news; but powerful counter-arguments can be advanced that the newspaper exists mainly to sell goods, to supplement the entertainments industry, and to influence public opinion. These functions naturally overlap, but one can at least identify them.

The content of newspapers can be studied in Raymond Williams' Communications *(Chatto & Windus, 1966), in which an illuminating set of tables analyses the major journals. Advertising normally accounts for a third of the space in the national newspapers. (Exceptions are the* Daily Sketch, *which carries rather little advertising, and the* Daily Telegraph, *which carries a great deal.) The rest is editorial matter. Much of this is straight entertainment. But much of it relates directly to current events of some importance, and it is worth while examining the newspapers' relationship to news. A newspaper is a forum for warring interests, and several factors can be identified. The newspaper itself holds views on public affairs,*

5

which it offers overtly in its editorials. It may also advance its views more subtly, in the selection and emphasis of certain news items. Alternative views may be advanced in the correspondence columns, representing at least in theory the general public. In printing certain news stories, official 'leaks', etc., the newspaper acts necessarily as an instrument of Government whether it will or no. Finally, the newspaper has a vital interest in news, however little suited this may be to the policies of its own editorial authority, Government, or anyone else. A newspaper is not a simple affair.

The role of the newspaper in influencing public opinion decisively is bound to be debatable. For example, it is often asserted that there has been no campaign, confined to a portion of the Press, to achieve a major political victory since 1916. In that year, Northcliffe's assault on the Asquith administration played a leading part in bringing the Government down. As recently as 1951, the Daily Mirror *achieved a significant success: its Election Day headline, 'Whose finger on the trigger?' is usually credited with limiting to tiny proportions the Conservative majority. Nowadays, however, the competition of TV and radio reduces the impact of the Press. Still, a national newspaper may commit itself to sustained advocacy of causes in a way impossible to radio and TV. The* Daily Express *has consistently opposed British entry to the Common Market; the* Guardian *has consistently urged successive British Governments to take a firm stand against the policies of South Africa. Any Government knows that on certain great issues, powerful organs of the Press will be ranged for or against it. The Government must weigh the risks of policies attacked by the Press, and imperfectly understood by the public. Moreover, the major issues are sometimes so complex (the Government Pension scheme, the Common Market agricultural policies) that nothing less than repeated exposition through article and editorial, sustained over a period of many months, is sufficient to enlighten the public. Only the Press can do this job. Thus the Press, both as reporter and interpreter of contemporary events, retains a vital role in educating the public. It is in this, and not as the vehicle for a Press Lord's campaign, that the capacity of the Press to influence public opinion lies.*

The latest circulation figures provide the basic data for study; of particular interest are the trends suggested by the comparisons they afford with those of past years. Certain points should be noted before the figures are interpreted, for there were several important internal changes in the national Press during the 1960's. The Daily Herald *metamorphosed into the* Sun: The Times *changed its character considerably, having now a much broader appeal than of old. This is reflected in its increased circulation figures. Generally, it is convenient to regard the daily Press as having three tiers, quality, middle and tabloid: and the overall story of the 1960's has been that the qualities* (Times, Telegraph, Guardian) *have increased their circulation steadily; the tabloids* (Mirror and Sketch) *have more than held their own; and the middle newspapers* (Express, Mail, and Sun) *have steadily lost ground. The quality Sundays* (Sunday Times, Observer, and Sunday Telegraph) *are also flourishing. The main difficulty in interpreting the latest circulation figures lies in assessing the importance of the aftermath of devaluation* (November 1967) *in 1968 and 1969. Undoubtedly, the financial climate had an adverse effect on newspaper circulation. How far these economic pressures operate against some, or all of the newspapers, time alone will tell. Overall, the latest statistics point to a slight but continued dwindling in the sales of daily newspapers* (though not of the Sundays, which more resemble magazines). *But this overall dwindling is of much less importance than the changing relationships within the Press.*

Lord Devlin discusses the principles whereby the Press seeks to impose standards upon its own operation. We then consider some of the larger questions of influencing the public which are raised, in part, by the Press, but not confined to it. Jeremy Tunstall describes the organization of an advertising agency. The restraints under which advertisers labour are most importantly embodied in 'The British Code of Advertising Practice'. No discussion of advertising practice makes sense unless it is related to the standards which the advertisers themselves formally adopt. The schools of thought within the profession are described by Mr Tunstall; clearly, no body of received advertising opinion exists. Martin Mayer's account of the mechanics of creating an advertisement reveals plainly that it is far from an *exact science. Advertising firms operate successfully on a variety of philosophies, and a good advertisement is a blend of creative intuition, professionalism, and market research. Of late years, some of the rancour has evaporated from the anti-advertising campaigns; many people nowadays seem to regard advertisements as a minor art form, and take a connoisseur's interest in them. They concern us here as experiments in communication. The point about advertisements is that they do, broadly, succeed. The relationship between product sales and advertising is absolutely established. If a given product is simultaneously marketed nationally, and advertised in one area only, sales will normally be higher in that area than in the rest of the country. An individual's reaction to advertising is unpredictable; the combined reactions of many individuals are much more predictable. Still, there is such a thing as an advertising campaign failure. (It is said that the great Edsel fiasco of the late 1950's cost Ford's close on $200 million.) Advertising agencies prosper and wane as they are judged to be efficient predictors of public reaction. We can regard advertising as large-scale, empirical research in communication.*

1 Table: Latest circulation figures for British National newspapers

Circulation (in thousands) of national newspapers

		Average net sales per publishing day 1 Jan. to 30 June 69	July-Dec. 1968	Jan.-June 1968	July-Dec. 1967	Jan.-June 1967	July-Dec. 1966	Jan.-June 1966	1964	1962
Quality dailies	The Times	437	415	401	364	334	290	273	255	253
	Daily Telegraph	1380	1379	1407	1400	1384	1352	1354	1319	—
	The Guardian	293	268	281	281	289	280	283	275	264
	Financial Times	172	163	156	148	150	148	152	152	137
Middle dailies	Daily Express	3732	3787	3853	3948	3963	4003	3954	4233	4288
	Daily Mail	1993	2039	2095	2145	2191	2255	2381	2412	2548
	The Sun	951	1009	1066	1131	1161	1228	1248	—	—
Popular dailies	Daily Mirror	4924	4949	5034	5282	5222	5187	5078	5018	4610
	Daily Sketch	871	886	915	886	871	865	849	885	954
Quality Sundays	Sunday Times	1454	1440	1461	1501	1512	1366	1360	1245	1117
	Observer	879	854	903	908	902	886	876	756	719
	Sunday Telegraph	753	747	713	704	651	659	641	658	—
Popular Sundays	News of the World	6228	6131	6191	6274	6149	6121	6184	6238	6464
	The People	5455	5427	5533	5608	5572	5538	5583	5584	5538
	Sunday Express	4235	4206	4236	4268	4219	4195	4168	4267	4366
	Sunday Mirror	5009	5015	5138	5350	5264	5264	5174	5077	5183

2 From: The Press and the People 13th Annual Report of the Press Council, 1966

THE SIX PILLARS OF PRESS COUNCIL SUCCESS

Inaugurating the annual conference of the Commonwealth Press Union in London in June, Lord Devlin named six factors which he deemed to be essential to the creation and proper working of a Press Council. He was speaking to representatives of many countries whose interests are not yet served by an institution such as the British Press Council.

Lord Devlin said:

The first factor is, of course, that there should be a general acceptance by the press itself that it is a desirable thing to have. This is certainly not something that goes without saying. There will be, as there would be in any profession, powerful voices raised against control of any sort. Many highminded men in the newspaper world will feel that even voluntary control is the thin end of the wedge and that there must be no tampering at all with the right to free expression in the printed word won by our ancestors only after a long fight against authority. The resolve to create a Press Council in this country was not taken easily or without outside pressure. But if the Press Council has, in the first twelve years of its existence, succeeded in dispelling the notion that its activities are akin to censorship and in satisfying both press and public that it seeks to hold the balance evenly between them, it may have set a pattern that it will now be easier to adopt.

The second factor is that the government of the country concerned, whatever form it takes, must be responsive to public opinion and must accept that the press has a constitutional part to play in the formation and expression of opinion. This means something more than lip service to the freedom of the press. It means that the public man who may resent criticism as unfair and ill-informed—and sometimes rightly so, for the critic is not always right—must be prepared to tolerate it as part of the process to which he is subject. He must accept publicity when he does not want it in the same spirit as he takes it when he wants and needs it. All this was excellently expressed by Mr Harold Macmillan when he was Prime Minister and speaking in the House of Commons in one of the debates on the press:

> The press has a right—and I think it would say a duty—to find out the truth, to publish it and comment on it as it thinks fit. That is its right, and I think we all feel that the advantages of a free press far outweigh any of its disadvantages. Naturally, like any right, this has a corresponding obligation.

The third factor is that the press must accept what Mr Macmillan rightly called its corresponding obligation. This means that there must be standards of conduct to which the press conforms. This does not necessarily mean a written code or rules that are enforceable by pains and penalties. But it does mean that the individual journalist cannot decide for himself the standards which he chooses to observe. A great newspaperman once said that a journalist's code should be in his own heart. If that means that he can decide every question of journalistic ethics for himself, it is not the sort of acceptance of 'corresponding obligation' that will satisfy the public. If every citizen were allowed to behave according to his own lights, there would be no room for the law and the State would be run on anarchical principles. No man can be allowed to be a law unto himself and the public will not accept, and cannot be expected to accept, that in this respect the journalist is more virtuous than the ordinary citizen.

The function of the Press Council is to settle standards. There need not be formal pains and penalties provided that there is general willingness to observe the standards that are settled. I think that in the British press, as a whole, there is.

I think that many cases of misbehaviour in the past have been due, not to a policy on the part of newspapers to behave as they like so long as it is not punishable, as to an uncertainty as to what they could and could not do and to a determination by each newspaper to make sure that it went as far as any of its rivals, if not further. If a standard is clearly set and each journalist is given a reasonable certainty that it will be observed by his competitors, he will observe it too.

The fourth factor is that a newspaper accepts the obligations to publish adjudications of the Press Council against itself. There is no formal undertaking about this but there has grown up an unwritten rule. Since the first Council came into existence in 1953 there have been only three occasions in which this unwritten rule has been broken. I regard its general observance as essential. In some sense it is a penalty—and sometimes rather a disagreeable one—which an offending newspaper has to pay. But its more important aspect is that it is necessary to satisfy the public in a way in which rebukes privately administered would never do, that standards are being observed and that there is a measure of public redress for those who are aggrieved by press behaviour. If a newspaper offends in what it publishes, it offends publicly; the redress must be public also.

The fifth factor is that the public is represented on the Press Council. It is perhaps going too far to class this as essential, but it is, I think, very important and very desirable. Other professions—medicine and the law, architects and estate agents and so on—can regulate their conduct according to purely professional standards. But the press helps to form and to express public opinion; and it is therefore important that its standards should take public opinion into account. Professional men, however upright, can easily fall into the error of judging complaints against themselves too narrowly, the press must not run the risk of that. The press is free because the public as a whole want it to be free. This inevitably means that the public is concerned in the way in which its freedom is exercised. This concern can be adequately expressed through a minority membership, which offers no threat of domination. There is also the practical advantage that a body on which the public is represented can assert publicly the rights and duties of the press with greater authority than a purely professional body could wield.

This brings me to the sixth and last factor. The Press Council in Britain is a body whose function it is to stand up for the freedom and rights of the press as well as to censure misconduct. To censure misconduct effectively it needs the support and respect of the press and it will obtain that much more readily if, in the words of its Constitution, it seeks to preserve the established freedom of the British press as well as to maintain its character in accordance with the highest professional and commercial standards. The Council must never allow itself to become merely a tribunal which convicts or acquits.

3   From: The Advertising Man by Jeremy Tunstall

1. Organization

In any agency the artists and copywriters are important, and they make up one-fifth of all employees. Although there is only one copywriter to every three artists, the copywriters are, on the whole, more important. This is due partly to historical reasons. In the days of space-broking, around the turn of the century, agencies began to employ a few copywriters as an additional service; in America a copywriter called John E. Kennedy was proclaiming that advertising was 'salesmanship in print'. By the time of the First World War the idea was firmly established in both England and America that advertising was also salesmanship in pictures. In 1909 Gordon Selfridge's spectacular campaign for the opening of the new shop in Oxford Street showed how illustrations could dominate full-page advertisements on the front page of the *Daily Mail* and in other newspapers. Yet copy had come first, and in 1920 the typical London advertising agency had a 'Copy department' which included the art studio.

The artists and copywriters in an agency follow a fairly rigid brief which is worked out by the account executive and his account supervisor in consultation with the client and with other agency departments, such as media, marketing and research. The brief is called the 'creative platform' and lays down the general kind of advertising which is required, what sort of media it will appear in, to what sort of people it will appeal, and the general type of message required. The senior creative people have a say in drawing up this platform, but the ordinary copywriter or artist does not; he merely works from it.

The first stage is to make rough advertisements with sketches and headlines, and perhaps some words of 'body copy'. These roughs then go forward for discussion in the agency; no more polished work is attempted until the client has agreed.

The final copy is written by copywriters inside the agency; but final art work is usually done outside; fairly detailed layouts are produced by agency artists, which after being approved by the client, are sent with specific instructions to an independent art or photographic studio, or in the case of television to a commercial film company. It is uneconomical to produce finished art work inside the agency, because a very wide range of work is required which can be more efficiently provided by specialized outsiders. Agency artists are mainly specialists in sketching and layout; senior agency artists are almost entirely administrators, and an agency art department of any size employs people whose sole job is to commission final art work from outside artists and photographers.

This highly specialized organization, and the system under which an agency artist tells an outside artist in considerable detail —down to sizes of figures, shades of colours, and so on—how to do a piece of art work, are indications of the rigid control exerted over individual expression in advertising art. The process of producing copy, on the other hand, is not split up in the same manner. An agency copywriter works on a copy assignment from the inception of the creative platform right through to the last comma on the final copy which goes into the advertisement. Although artists are indispensable, copywriters play a more central role in agencies.

Both artists and copywriters agree that in the vast majority of cases copywriters have the first idea and take the initiative in choosing the creative theme. In the case of certain products such as lipstick, which inevitably demand a picture of a face—the artist may take the initiative; but usually it is a copywriter who has the first idea of showing a woman wheeling a pram, a little girl talking to her father, or whatever it may be. Artists and copy people agree that the reason why the copywriter usually takes the initiative is because his job is words and ideas. One copy-writer said that if an artist wants to take the initiative he just tells him to go right ahead, but the artist is usually unable to think of anything.

Any artist who works in advertising must accept that he is not free to do what he likes, and artists seem to prefer taking sugges-tions from copywriters rather than from other people. As one copywriter said, 'We've got common enemies—the account men in the agency, and the client'. Copywriters insist that artists must be handled carefully, but their attitude implies that artists are easier to handle than are account executives and some other groups in the agency.

With any particular account the advertising message may vary slightly from medium to medium and from season to season, but it is usually regarded as essential to have only one major theme

14

running at one time. One art director spoke about a finished advertisement for a piece of kitchen equipment. It had been discovered through market research that housewives were worried that the product would become quickly out of date; the creative platform laid down that housewives must be persuaded this would not happen. The copywriter who was working on the account suggested a picture of a little girl, with copy saying that the product would still be up to date and efficient when the girl had grown up. This theme was used in all the advertisements. Indeed, the little girl was even introduced in person to the company's salesmen at the sales conference arranged to show them the new advertising campaign.

A good deal of controversy surrounds the question of the best organization of creative departments. In most small agencies there are at the top a copy chief and an art director of equal status, and they assign individual copywriters and artists to accounts as they think necessary. In all but the small agencies the artists are split into art groups, each group containing a number of artists who have a batch of accounts assigned to them. Copywriters also, especially in large agencies, are split into groups, each of which is under a 'copy chief'. A more centralized type of organization, again common in large agencies, has several creative directors, and each of these has directly subordinate to him an art director and a copy chief.

Television advertising is usually handled by a separate department and since for many agencies television takes up between a quarter and a half of billings, the television department can be quite large. The key people in a television department are the 'television producers'. These men have a general responsibility for television commercials made for the agency's clients. When the film is actually being made by a film director (usually working for an outside film company) it is the television producer who represents the agency's interest, and is responsible for much of the detailed planning of the film, such as deciding on the sort of film set that is to be used. He may also take part in the preliminary planning and writing of the commercial.

However, at this point the role of the television producer becomes rather uncertain. When the client approves the making of a commercial he is normally shown a 'storyboard', which is a series of sketches with the words written underneath. Copywriters usually take a part in preparing the storyboard, but some copywriters are inexperienced in this medium and the television producer plays a more important role. On the other hand some copywriters regard themselves as experts in writing for television and they may even supervise such details as recording of music, in addition to attending the actual shooting of the film.

In most agencies artists play a part in the early thinking about commercials, and the film director who finally makes the film may find the artist's visual ideas more intrusive than the ideas of the copywriter. However, some clients with a lot of television experience are prepared to accept merely a written film script and in this case it may be that no agency artist is involved at all.

These different approaches to the making of television commercials are signs that in this field the creative organization is—as the creative people are fond of saying—in a state of flux. Indeed, organization charts in creative departments seem to indicate even less than they do elsewhere. One large agency has five 'creative directors' each of whom in theory has copy chiefs and art directors reporting to him; however, one of the copy chiefs claimed that these creative directors in fact carried out quite other functions in the agency, while he actually reported direct to an account director, a member of the agency Board.

The individual artist or copywriter may always work with the same few creative people, or he may work on each different account with a different set of people. Each system has advantages and disadvantages, because the desired objects are to some extent contradictory; while the agency wants of its creative people strong, fresh, clear ideas and work, it also wants efficiency, punctuality and other such virtues.

But whatever the system under which they are organized, artists and copywriters stand in the same general relation to clients, account executives, and the agency's service departments. They are always being asked to create advertisements to a more or less rigid specification, drawn up by someone else.

4   From: The British Code of Advertising Practice

This Code, which has the support of the organizations listed below, has been set up for the guidance of all advertisers, advertising agencies, those controlling advertising media and suppliers of various advertising services.

The Code requires that all advertising should be legal, clean, honest and truthful; and defines practices agreed to be undesirable by the organizations which have subscribed to it. As the function of advertising is advocacy, it is acknowledged that within the provisions of the Code, advertisers should be free to put forward the best case for the acceptance of their products by consumers.

THE ADVERTISING CONTROL SYSTEM

The standards established under the Code are administered by the Advertising Standards Authority (ASA), the Code of Advertising Practice Committee (the CAP Committee) and the Advertising Investigation Department of the Advertising Association (AID), together with the Copy Committees of the sponsoring bodies.

The Advertising Standards Authority

The Advertising Standards Authority is an independent body set up with the object of 'the promotion and enforcement throughout the U.K. of the highest standards of advertising in all media so as to ensure in co-operation with all concerned that no advertising contravenes or offends against these standards'. It also initiates or approves modifications to improve the Code and keep it up to date. Ten members are appointed by an independent Chairman to serve as individuals and not as representatives of any section or interest. Five members must be from outside the advertising industry, thus ensuring that, with the Chairman, there is an independent majority.

The Code of Advertising Practice Committee

The CAP Committee is responsible for the operation and interpretation of the Code of Advertising Practice. It is also responsible for the amendment and improvement of the Code itself (subject to ratification by ASA) to meet changing conditions; for resolving difficulties between members of the industry which may arise over the Code; for giving advice to ASA on the operation of the Code; for ensuring that the resulting policy is carried out effectively; and applying sanctions wherever necessary. The Committee also issues bulletins notifying changes in and advice on interpretation of the Code.

The Advertising Investigation Department

The Advertising Investigation Department is a service department of the Advertising Association, providing guidance and advice on copy matters. It is also the investigating body for both ASA and the CAP Committee, undertakes their research, investigation and reporting, and is responsible for the monitoring of advertisements in all media.

Copy Committees of Sponsoring Bodies
In addition to the centralized administration described above the individual sponsoring bodies have their own committees, responsible for securing the enforcement of the provisions of the Code.

Advice
When in any doubt as to the application of the Code, advertisers, advertising agencies and media are advised, in their own interests, to seek guidance from the Advertising Investigation Department or the appropriate sponsoring organization.

Sponsoring Organizations
The Code has the support of the following organizations, all of which are represented on the CAP Committee:

The Advertising Association
The British Direct Mail Advertising Association
The British Poster Advertising Association
The Direct Mail Producers Association
The Electrical Sign Manufacturers' Association
The Incorporated Society of British Advertisers
The Independent Television Companies Association
The Institute of Practitioners in Advertising
The Master Sign Makers' Association
The Newspaper Proprietors Association
The Newspaper Society
Periodical Publishers Association
The Proprietary Association of Great Britain
The Scottish Daily Newspaper Society
The Scottish Newspaper Proprietors Association
The Screen Advertising Association
The Solus Outdoor Advertising Association

It should be emphasized that the Code is an accepted minimum requirement and media copy committees and individual media (particularly television, which has statutory obligations) may impose additional requirements.

18

PART A

GENERAL

All advertising should be legal, clean, honest and truthful.

Scope

1.1 The Code is to be applied in the spirit as well as in the letter.

1.2 This part of the Code applies to all advertising. Special provisions also apply to medicines, treatments and appliances. (See Part B.)

Interpretation

2.1 The word 'advertisement' throughout this Code embraces all forms of advertising, including packaging, labelling, literature, catalogues and point of sale material.

2.2 The word 'product' includes services.

Content

3 Advertisements should not in any way bring advertising into contempt, offend against decency, or reduce public confidence in or weaken the acceptance of advertising as an essential service to industry and the public.

Misleading Descriptions and Claims

4.1 Advertisements should not contain any description, claim or illustration which is directly or by implication misleading about the product advertised or about its suitability for the purpose recommended.

4.2 Advertisements should not contain any reference which is likely to lead the public to assume that the product advertised, or any ingredient, has some special quality or property which cannot be established.

Scientific Terms and Statistics

5 Advertisements should not misuse scientific terms, statistics or quotations. In particular:

(a) scientific jargon and irrelevancies should not be used to make claims appear to have a scientific basis they do not possess

(b) statistics with a limited validity should not be presented in such a way as to imply that they are universally true.

Substantiation

6　Advertisements should not contain any description, claim or illustration which cannot be substantiated. Advertisers and advertising agencies should provide substantiation without delay when called upon to do so.

Appeals to fear

7　Advertisements should not without justifiable reason play on fear.

Superstition

8　Advertisements should not exploit the superstitious.

Knocking Copy

9　Advertisements should not discredit or unfairly attack other products or advertisements. In featuring product benefits, any comparison (either stated or implied) with other products should be fair, capable of substantiation and in no way misleading.

Imitation

10　Advertisements should not imitate the devices, copy, slogans or general layout of other advertisements in a way that is likely to mislead. Particular care should be taken in the packaging and labelling of goods to avoid confusion with other goods.

Comparative Prices

11　Advertisements should not contain actual or comparative prices and costs which are inaccurate or capable of misleading by distortion or undue emphasis.

Use of the word 'Free'

12　Advertisements should not describe goods or samples as 'free' unless the goods or samples are supplied at no cost or no extra cost (other than actual postage or carriage) to the recipient. A trial may be described as 'free' although the customer is expected to pay the cost of returning the goods, provided that the advertisement makes clear the customer's obligation to do so.

Guarantees

13　Advertisements should not contain the words 'guarantee', 'guaranteed', 'warranty' or 'warranted' or words having the same meaning, unless the full terms of the guarantee are clearly set out in the advertisement, or are supplied to the purchaser in writing at the point of sale or with the goods. In all cases the terms should include details of the remedial action open to the purchaser. No advertisement should contain a direct or implied reference to a guarantee which takes away or diminishes the statutory or common law rights of a purchaser, unless the manufacturer assumes a contractual responsibility to the purchaser in extent at least equivalent to such rights.

Testimonials
14.1 Advertisements should not contain any testimonial unless it is genuine, is not more than three years old, and is limited to the views of the person giving it.
14.2 Testimonials should not contain any statement or implication which would not be permitted in the text of the advertisement.

Safety
15 Advertisements should not without adequate justification depict or describe situations which show dangerous practices or a disregard for safety. Special care should be taken in advertisements directed towards or depicting children.

Advertisements addressed to Children
16 Advertisements addressed to children should not contain anything, whether in illustration or otherwise, which might result in harming them, physically, mentally or morally, or which exploits their credulity.

Advertisements presented in the style of News or Editorial
17 Advertisements should be so presented that they can be readily distinguished from news or editorial opinion.

Mail Order
18.1 Advertisements for goods offered by mail order should not be accepted unless:
   (a) the name of the advertiser is prominently displayed at the address given in the advertisement
   (b) adequate arrangements exist at that address for enquiries to be handled by a responsible person available on the premises during normal business hours

(c) samples of the goods advertised are made available there for public inspection and

(d) an undertaking has been obtained from the advertiser that money will be refunded in full to buyers who can show justifiable cause for dissatisfaction with their purchases or with delay in delivery.

18.2 Advertisers who offer goods by mail order should be prepared to meet any reasonable demand created by their advertising, and should be prepared to demonstrate or where practicable supply samples of the goods advertised to the media owners to whom their advertisements are submitted.

Direct Sale Advertising

19.1 Advertisements for goods supplied by direct sale (i.e. goods sold at the home by advertisers' representatives) should not be accepted without adequate assurances from the advertiser and his advertising agency:

(a) that the goods advertised will be supplied at the price stated in the advertisement within a reasonable time

(b) that supplies will be sufficient to meet likely demand

(c) that sales representatives when calling on persons responding to the advertisement will demonstrate and make available for sale the goods advertised.

19.2 The advertiser's intention to send a representative to call on persons responding to the advertisement must be clear from the advertisement or from the particulars subsequently supplied, and the respondent must be given an adequate opportunity of refusing any home visit.

Homework Schemes

20 Advertisements for homework schemes should not contain conditions which make unreasonable demands on the respondent. 'Homework Scheme' means a scheme in which an advertiser invites persons to make articles at home and promises or implies that payment will be made for finished articles.

Inertia Selling

21 Advertisements should not be accepted from advertisers who send the goods advertised, or additional goods, without authority from the recipient.

Instructional Courses

22.1 Advertisements offering courses of instruction should not promise or imply that persons completing such courses will obtain any particular employment or level of remuneration; nor offer unrecognized 'degrees' or qualifications.

22.2 Advertisements for correspondence courses in chiropody or any of the other auxiliary services covered by the Professions Supplementary to Medicine Act 1960 (i.e. Dietitians, Medical Laboratory Technicians, Occupational Therapists, Physiotherapists, Radiographers and Remedial Gymnasts) should not be accepted.

PART B

MEDICINES, TREATMENTS & APPLIANCES

(These paragraphs apply in addition to those in Part A.)

Interpretation

23 This part of the Code applies to the advertising to the public of medicines, treatments and appliances for the prevention or alleviation of any ailment, illness or disease. It does not apply to advertisements published by or under the authority of a Government Ministry or Department, nor to advertisements for medicines, treatments and appliances addressed directly to registered medical or dental practitioners, pharmacists, registered medical auxiliaries or nurses, sent direct or published in their respective professional or technical journals.

Cure

24 Advertisements should not contain any claim (directly or by implication) to extirpate any ailment, illness, disease or symptom of ill-health.

Illnesses requiring medical attention

25 Advertisements should not offer any medicine or treatment for serious diseases, conditions or complaints which need the attention of a registered medical practitioner.

Appeals to Fear

26 Advertisements should not contain any statement or illustration likely to induce fear on the part of the reader or viewer

that he is suffering, or may without treatment suffer, or suffer more severely, from an ailment, illness or disease.

Diagnosis or treatment by Correspondence
27 Advertisements should not contain any offer to diagnose or to treat any ailment, illness or disease, or symptoms of ill-health by correspondence; nor invite information in order to advise on or prescribe treatment by correspondence.

Money-back Offers
28 Advertisements should not contain any offer to refund money to dissatisfied users.

This paragraph does not apply to mail order advertising of medical appliances or therapeutic wearing apparel. (But see Part A, para 18.)

College, Hospital, Clinic, Institute, Laboratory
29 Advertisements should not contain any reference to a 'College', 'Hospital', 'Clinic', 'Institute', 'Laboratory' or similar establishment unless there exists a bona fide establishment corresponding to the description used.

Medical Statements, Trials and Tests
30.1 Advertisements should not contain any medical statement or reference to clinical or other trials or tests which cannot be substantiated by authoritative evidence.

30.2 No product with a name containing the term 'Doctor' or 'Dr' is acceptable unless the product was marketed under that name prior to 1st January, 1944.

Testimonials
31 Advertisements should not contain any testimonial given by a doctor who is not a registered British medical practitioner unless the advertisement makes it clear that the writer is not so registered.

Exaggerated Copy
32 Advertisements should not contain copy which is exaggerated by reason of the improper use of words, phrases or methods of presentation, e.g. the use of the words 'magic', 'magical', 'miracle', 'miraculous'.

'Natural' Remedies
33 Advertisements should not contain any false claim, direct or indirect, that a product is 'natural', 'nature's remedy' or the like.

24

Competitions

34 Advertisements for medicines, treatments and appliances should not contain any reference to a prize competition or similar scheme.

Slimming, Weight reduction, limitation or control

35 Advertisements should not contain any offer of any product or treatment for slimming (i.e. weight reduction, limitation or control) which:

(a) is in itself likely to lead to harmful effects
(b) is not directly associated with the following of a properly designed diet.

Bust Developers

36 Advertisements for preparations and devices purporting to promote enlargement of the bust are not permissible.

Products offered particularly to women

37 Advertisements should not suggest or imply that any products, medicines or treatments offered therein will induce miscarriage.

Sexual weakness, Premature ageing, Loss of Virility

38 Advertisements should not suggest or imply that any product, medicine or treatment offered therein will promote sexual virility or be effective in treating sexual weakness, or habits associated with sexual excess or indulgence, or any ailment, illness or disease associated with such habits.

Hypnosis

39 Advertisements should not contain any offer to diagnose or treat conditions of ill-health by hypnosis.

Hair and scalp products and treatments

40 Advertisements relating to hair and scalp products and treatments should not contain:

(a) any offer of diagnosis by post or telephone or any claim or implication that the product or treatment advertised will do more than arrest loss of hair
(b) any particulars of establishments administering treatments for the hair and scalp other than the name, address, telephone number and hours of attendance. The types of treatment available may be mentioned

provided that there is no reference to specific conditions
for which such treatment is intended.

Haemorrhoids
41   Advertisements should not contain any offer of products
for the treatment of haemorrhoids unless the following
warning notice is contained in the directions for use on the
container itself or its labels: 'Persons who suffer from
haemorrhoids are advised to consult a doctor.'

Products offered for the relief of backache and rheumatic pains
42   Advertisements should not contain any claims for the relief
of backache and rheumatic pains based upon the urinary
antiseptic properties of the products advertised.

Vitamin Products
43   Advertisements should not contain any unqualified claims
that vitamins will give adequate protection against or treatment for virus infections, or unqualified statements that the
medical profession supports such claims.

5   From: The Advertising Man by Jeremy Tunstall

3. Hard or soft sell?

It should be an advantage to industry to be able to show that
there are other standards in advertising than purely commercial
ones.

Many industrialists are scarcely aware of the importance of an
advantageous public image that can be created for their
companies by typographical designers and art directors.—
Lord Snowdon (1963).

Nobody is very surprised today when *The Times* prints a special
supplement devoted to advertising art. Serious poster art in this
country is said to date from Frederick Walker's 'The Woman in
White' (1871) and Millais' 'Bubbles' (1886). Toulouse-Lautrec's
posters also had some immediate influence in Britain. Such

advertisements were atypical, but after posters like McKnight Kauffer's 'London Museum' of 1922 appeared, impressionist-style advertising art began to acquire a strong influence in Britain.

Since then the London Transport Executive has been a leading exponent of serious art in advertising. Between 1928 and 1936 London Transport used specially commissioned posters by Jacob Epstein, Rex Whistler, and Graham Sutherland. During the same period the Empire Marketing Board also employed serious artists, and pioneered in the field of the documentary film with its EMB Film Unit (which later became the Crown Film Unit).

More recently television commercials have provided a field in which the talents of distinguished film directors can be used. Such directors as Alexander McKendrick, Jack Clayton, and Karel Reisz have all made commercial films.

Nevertheless, the use of work by such distinguished artists remains extremely atypical of general advertising practice. A more potent influence—especially on the artistic aspirations of agency creative workers—is exerted by various prize competitions for advertisements. The most important of the British competitions are the Layton Awards. In recent years the Mather and Crowther agency has been easily the most successful in winning awards—for clients such as the Milk Publicity Council, the Egg Marketing Board, Player's, Singer and Shell. It is difficult to say how much prestige an agency gains from awards; W. S. Crawford, another agency which wins art awards, has not been rising in the 'billings league' recently. But Mather and Crowther has a reputation as the leading creative agency, and creative people in other agencies think very highly of these advertisements.

The Layton Awards are primarily for 'graphic effectiveness', not sales impact. Prizes are also given for product packaging (which agencies often design) and here again sales appeal is only one of the factors—among others like product protection, graphic design, and ingenuity of construction—which are taken into account by the judges.

Advertising prizes, and the seductive influence they may have on agency creative staffs, are not without critics, who point out that advertising is supposed to be selling goods, not producing beautiful designs. John Metcalf of the Hobson, Bates, agency puts it like this:

I think that awards take us away from what our job is. They take us away from the judgment of effectiveness and take our people away from creativeness.

27

The more we alienate ourselves from our clients in this way, the more we are disassociating ourselves from industry. If we are not concerned with profits and we go on listening to this siren song of awards, then we might as well sit down.

The judges for the Layton Awards, however, tend to make precisely the opposite criticism—that even prize-winning advertisements often fail to reach a high standard of design. For this reason prizes in some sections are not awarded at all. One of the judges in the 1961 competition had this to say:

> No one who has seen the submissions to the Layton Awards can have any doubt that the design of British advertising is very far from being satisfactory. The overall impression is of a most careful avoidance of any freshness of approach and originality. *Do what your competitor does, only more so* seems to be the generally accepted basic principle, and the fundamental thinking follows a very limited number of well-trodden grooves without ever doubting their validity.

This is the opinion of Mr George Him, of the Society of Industrial Artists; the Layton Awards jury contains four representatives of such bodies, and only one judge representing the advertisers.

Despite such strong differences of opinion about the standard and relevance of design in British Advertising, there is a considerable degree of consensus about the influence of American creative advertising. Those who deplore the low standard of creativity in Britain, those who like unpretty but hard-selling advertising tested by copy research, and creative people who feel their status in advertising should be higher, all these conflicting groups tend to look towards America with approval.

British advertising people normally see only a tiny fraction of American advertising—a few television commercials, such as the Chevrolet one which was given the television Grand Prix at the Cannes international commercial film festival in 1963, media and agency house advertising in the American trade press, and prestige advertising in *Esquire, Life* and the *New Yorker*. Perhaps even more admired are the collections of prize-winning advertisements chosen by the Art Directors' Club of New York, which are even less typical of American advertising in general. Of eleven advertisements which were awarded the Art Directors' Club Medal in 1961 four were for magazines, one was an agency house advertisement and two were for an imported product.

One ex-copywriter has said on the BBC that creative ideas for

advertising products in Britain are taken from American magazines of two or three years ago. An example of this is the
'Drinka pinta milka day' campaign which first appeared in
British posters in April 1959, and seems to be based on a campaign
launched in 1956 by the United Fruit Company—'Havabanana',
'Drinkabanana', 'Mashabanana', 'How to sling the new banana-
slang', etc. Indeed, this American campaign seems also to have
influenced another, quite separate British campaign—'Unzip a
banana'.

Many creative people in the agencies say that advertisers are
underestimating the intelligence of the public. David Ogilvy, the
leading exponent of 'image' advertising, says, 'The consumer is
not a moron. She is *your wife*. And she is grown-up.'

An English artist, Kenneth Bromfield, agrees:

> From any cross-section of ads the general advertiser's attitude
> would seem to be: If you are a lousy, smelly, idle, under-
> privileged and over-sexed status-seeking neurotic moron, give
> me your money. . . . Why is our advertising so bloody awful?
> Mainly because it is lacking in interest, ideas and design. And
> repetitive to the point of boredom.

While copywriters and artists complain that advertisers under-
estimate the intelligence of the public, there is a contrary argument which says that creative people, in so far as they care at all,
overestimate the public's intelligence. Artists, in particular, are
accused of living in ivory towers, of being remote from reality, and
of having grown up in the sheltered world of art schools. Copywriters are generally considered to be more down to earth than
artists, but Brian McCabe, the head of Foote, Cone and Belding,
in London, expressed a popular view when he attacked copywriters for their 'long words, long sentences, and long hair'.
McCabe suggested that copywriters should take their summer
holidays in Butlin's camps rather than on the Riviera.

All agency men agree that while advertisements must be read,
merely attracting attention is not enough because advertisements
must also sell; moreover what was once an effective approach must
eventually by its very success and usage become boring. The
basic message is agreed to be important, but since no hard and
fast rules exist, or can exist, for arriving at it, every case must
be thrown open to judgment and dispute.

If one wants to sell a product to manual workers should one
show manual workers in the advertisements and use colloquial
language? One argument says yes, but the other says it is best

always to aim above reality—to show the white-collar man the manual worker would like to be, and the elegant model the housewife dreams of becoming. Similar debates centre around endorsements of products by celebrities. In America this type of approach is so much used that there exists a special firm called Endorsements, Inc.—'a unique organization in the field of bringing together the advertiser and the endorser'. In Germany, by contrast, this type of advertising is virtually unknown. In Britain endorsements are used to some extent; they presumably have the advantage that really famous personalities attract attention. But are the testimonials believable? The field is open once again to opinion.

The same goes for humour. Really funny advertisements certainly do attract attention. But opponents of humour in advertising say that the consumer is being asked to part with his money and this is no laughing matter. Another point here is that humour is a standard weapon of the seducer.

The basic argument about creative approaches to advertising concerns the relative merits of 'hard-sell' and 'soft-sell'. The hard-sell approach follows the advertising tradition dating from the beginning of this century which insists that the consumer should be given a 'reason why' she ought to buy the product: Mrs Jones buys detergent X because it washes whiter than new. The soft-sell approach relies on a more subtle and indirect message: Miss Jones goes for a beautiful walk in the country with her fiancé and relaxes afterwards with product Y. In some cases there can be little dispute as to whether hard- or soft-sell approach should be used. Detergents are utilitarian and are presented through a hard-sell approach; cosmetics are luxury products appealing to vanity and are sold with soft-sell vague promises of romance. But in many cases people will not agree as to which is the better course.

In general, copywriters and artists are against the traditional hard-sell approach; it does not demand interesting art work, it depends on crude, bold typography, the copy is straightforward and dull. Creative people complain that hard-sell advertising is not only unimaginative but gives the product a cheap image; they tend to advocate a subtle attempt to build up a 'quality image' over a long time span. Soft-sell image advertising calls for striking illustrations, and requires of the copywriter an indirect approach, which demands a subtle solution.

Whereas hard-sell advertising gives the consumer a 'reason why', soft-sell advertising proceeds from a different premise.

Advocates of the soft-sell point out that there is often little difference between the competing products in a field, so there is no genuine, rational reason for buying one brand rather than another. The soft-sell approach is to appeal indirectly, tangentially, to the emotions—and to establish a connection between product X and some symbol of romance, or prestige. As soft-sell advertising rejects appeals to reason in favour of appeals to emotions, copywriters who persistently argue for a soft-selling approach are calling for an appeal to the consumers' irrationality. They inevitably make a sharp distinction between themselves— creative workers in advertising—and the consumers. Other people in advertising, including clients and account executives, who are not so committed to subtle creative work, may be forgiven for finding a basic confusion in these arguments. The creative people often appear to be saying two contradictory things: firstly that the intelligence of the consumer is underestimated by advertising and secondly, that advertising should aim less at rational appeals, more at appeals to the emotions. Thus in advocating soft-sell advertising creative people find themselves in a paradoxical position; they are also open to accusations of setting themselves apart from the mass of the public.

6   From: Madison Avenue U.S.A. by Martin Mayer

Nothing could be more atypical of normal advertising procedure, of course, than the introduction of a new automobile. The workaday copywriter spends the great bulk of his time writing new words to fit old themes for products which have been around some time. Every agency will turn out a certain number of new campaigns every year—but the need for something fresh and different is still rare enough so that it causes great agitation in an agency, a vast flap of overtime work and nervous indigestion, every time the demand is made.

The basic creative job is the discovery of what is variously called the 'sales' or 'purchase' proposition, the 'platform', or the 'campaign theme', and there are a dozen different ways of handling it. At Foote, Cone the primary responsibility lies with the creative group, whose members start work with a general meeting at which the copy chief outlines the nature of the problem and the factual frame within which a solution must be found. Members of the group then go off and think about it, and a second meeting develops one or more campaign themes which look promising. Ads are prepared in rough form (a good art director can turn out in fifteen minutes a rough illustration which suggests everything that will be found in the finished advertisement, down to the sweat on the glasses which hold the cold drinks), and a week later the group meets again to look over what sort of advertising the suggested themes have produced. 'We go down the line,' says Melcon Tashian, head of Foote, Cone's New York art department, 'picking all the ads apart—is this headline right? should we have two children here, or a mother and one child? After we've talked over all the rough ads, we'll usually find a single *direction* we want to proceed in.' As an ordinary matter, the account representative does not participate in these meetings of the creative group, only after the group has decided on the direction, and made some advertising to demonstrate where the direction leads, does the copy chief call him in, to 'show him the philosophy,' Tashian says, not intolerantly, 'and sell him what we've done'.

At Ted Bates & Company the development of the Unique Selling Proposition is the responsibility of the copywriters alone, though they may call in help from the world of medical research if they feel the need for it; since virtually all the heads of the agency are still working copywriters, responsibility lies mainly in their hands. In David Ogilvy's agency, similarly, the individual copywriter, sitting alone at his desk, is the man in charge. 'Planning a campaign,' says David McCall, the very young second-in-command of Ogilvy's copy department, 'I sit down with all the facts I can get on the product, soak all that up, absorb it—except maybe the very technical stuff that you can't use with the public. Then I get old *U.S. Cameras*, because I find looking at pictures a great stimulus to ideas; and I get the Watkins book and the *Printers' Ink* book on the Hundred Greatest Advertisements, because I'm a great cribber. You've got to know the precedents—it's just like the law, in a way. So you sit leafing through with no ideas, but with your head full of information about the product, and something's bound to hit. At least you hope it will. Then, before giving the idea to the art director, or writing the copy, you might take it to the account executive or you might not, depending.' It can be even more simple than that; Norman, Craig & Kummel's Kay Daly, for example, gets all the facts and then 'forgets them. Instead, I think, if I were a woman —which I am—what would make me want to buy this product?'

At McCann-Erickson, on the other hand, the emphasis is on the marketing experts and the research department. A product group chaired by the account supervisor and containing six to eight senior men (of whom two will come from the creative department) sifts through the factual material and arrives at a 'purchase proposition' which is written down in full detail, with explanations, as a 'start-work report'. This report is the agency's plan of attack on the client's overall problem, and though it is built around the campaign theme, it will contain much more than that. 'Normally,' says Larry Deane, head of McCann's management service department, 'it takes twenty weeks to prepare a plan.' The full report then goes up to a 'marketing plans board', on which there are two representatives of the creative department, which accepts the plan or revises it. By and large, McCann copywriters do not come into the job until after the purchase proposition has been approved by the client; they are, as Anthony Hyde puts it, 'left free to develop the proper "audience strategy", which is the *real* creative problem'. In other words, they make the ads rather than think up the ideas. (Or so, at any rate, flows the chart; in fact, McCann's creative procedures are not greatly different from those at other agencies. As creative director Jack Tinker puts it, 'When David McCall sits down with all the facts he can get, he is doing just what our people do when they sit down with the "start-work report".')

The Thompson company, inevitably, occupies a middle ground. Discussion of the 'sales proposition' begins at a meeting of account supervisor, account representative and creative group head. According to group head Ed Robinson, the account supervisor opens the meeting with the words, 'We have X amount of advertising to do next year for this client, and these are the problems.' Long discussion by the three men produces one or more sales propositions, which the group head relays down to his copywriters and artists, who may or may not like the proposed ideas. Comments from the creative staff are carried by the group head to a second meeting of the three top men, and a single sales proposition is agreed upon—subject to further discussion after one of Thompson's *ad hoc* Review Boards has examined the idea, and after Jim Young, who comes in for two weeks every two months to act as 'senior consultant' and look over all the agency's major advertising campaigns, has given the account group the benefit of his forty-two years' experience as a working copywriter. Finally decision, as always at Thompson, rests in the hands of the account supervisor, a power which is allowed to him, in the true Thompson tradition, on condition that he does not get ornery about it.

The original source of the basic selling idea may be outside the agency; these days, it is no surprise if the campaign theme is something which has been worked up by a research firm. Those researchers who are in business to discover what 'motivates' consumers will automatically, as part of the service, suggest campaign themes to their clients. Thus, Ernest Dichter found that most women refused to bake cakes because of 'fear of failure', and bought cake mixes to eliminate mischance rather than to save time; he recommended to General Mills and BBDO[1] the campaign built around Betty Crocker's 'I Guarantee', and featuring illustrations of very simple cakes which a housewife might see herself producing. (Actually, BBDO was doing its own research, leading to the same results, at the same time.) Alfred Politz will compare 'issue values' for his clients to find one best advertising theme; Politz told Coca-Cola and McCann-Erickson that Coke's great asset was its omnipresence, the fact that everybody and every place served it, it was irrefutably part of the American scene and the advertising should stress its comparability to apple pie as the primary American gastronomic phenomenon. And not infrequently, of course, the client knows just which sales argument for his product he wants to have the agency push, and he is not going to be talked out of it. Once Leo Burnett had made Marlboro a big seller with his masculine image campaign, the Philip Morris Company demanded similar advertising for its Parliament and Philip Morris brands—and could not be dissuaded.

2

'Once you've found a Unique Selling Proposition,' says Rosser Reeves of Ted Bates, 'any good copywriter can write a good ad. The rest is just wordsmithing. Not that wordsmithing isn't important—we pay a fortune for copywriting talent. But five top copywriters might turn out five entirely different ads, all good, from a single USP—while all the wordsmithing in the world won't move the product off the shelf if the claim isn't right.'

[1] BBDO—Batten, Barton, Durstine & Osborn.

Most copy people would take a different tack; admitting the primacy of the sales pitch when there is a significantly new claim to be made, they would argue that in most fields where advertising is heavy everybody is making pretty much the same pitch, and it is the creative man's ability to present the claim most effectively which pulls his client into the lead. The decision about the basic sales argument may have been taken out of the copywriter's hands by an executive committee, but the copywriter's talent for ways and means is still, in this view, the determining factor in a campaign's success or failure. It was easy enough for Foote, Cone to decide that Colgate had pre-empted the bad-breath business and Gleem the cavities business, so Pepsodent should stick to cleaning the teeth; but without copywriter and jazz hobbyist Don Williams to write 'You'll Wonder Where the Yellow Went' the Pepsodent claim would never have drawn much public attention. Similarly, Young & Rubicam, like every other agency, knew that beer drinking was a way to let your hair down; but it took a creative man's intuition to come up with Bert and Harry Piel.

Basically, the advertising copywriter and the advertising artist work to make the product claim believable, in terms of the product itself and in terms of the people who will use it. Agencies (mindful, perhaps, of Claude Hopkins' 'Washed With Live Steam') make sure that every copywriter who works on an account has had a thorough tour of the client's factory; these excursions rarely produce a new claim, but they almost always give the copywriter an added command of detail, which adds conviction to his writing. (They also give him some respect for the client, which he does not always have before he sees how complicated the client's business is.) For the same reason, the copywriter is also expected to master most of the technical literature in the product field; 'working on toothpastes', says Thompson's Dick Neff, 'I've read a shelf of dentistry books as long as my arms'.

Sometimes these one-man research jobs, done by people with a copywriter's intuition, lead to changes in the product itself, because the creative department feels the sales pitch will be more believable if these changes are made. Thus, Thompson urged the J. B. Williams Company to make its shaving cream yellow, which would 'demonstrate' the lanolin content. When new products are in question, many agencies like to sit in on the planning from the laboratory stage, hoping to build in a feature which will make a claim more believable. Norman, Craig & Kummel suggested to Revlon the idea of silicon in a hand lotion, and the name Silicare, to make a medical sales argument more convincing. Sometimes, in browsing around a product field, the copywriters will find a completely new idea for a product feature, which they think can be sold. Random investigations in toothpaste brought Thompson's creative staff to a man who had invented a tube nozzle which coloured the sides of the emerging ribbon of toothpaste. Without even telling Lever Brothers what they were up to, the copywriters and artists picked a name (Stripe), designed a box, and laid out in rough form an advertising campaign on the slogan 'Looks Like Fun, Cleans Like Crazy'. Then they took the package to Lever Brothers, which most unexpectedly found itself with a new product.

Most of the time the shrewd copywriter works on the technical end of a product not to explore its manufacture but to find additional use values for it—to suggest, for example, that Q-tips are good, clean substitutes for fingers in children's finger painting. A man who worked intimately for some years with Jim Young on the Thompson Review Board recalls that Young's first question on a food account was always, 'Can you think of some new *way* to eat it?' BBDO's Jean Rindlaub applied exactly this approach to the Campbell's Soup account. 'We didn't have any share-of-market problem,' she says. 'What we had to do was increase the consumption of soup. We went out into the market and talked about soup—everybody had already heard about soup. The motivational research wasn't much help; it just said soup was warm and comforting. So we began having fun with it, myself, all the girls in the office. We had soup in mugs, soup for breakfast, soup on the rocks, soup shakes, scrambled eggs with soup, chilled tomato soup from a pitcher. We had more damn fun,' Mrs Rindlaub says, making her black eyes dance in the house-motherly manner she cultivates as a personnel technique with her girl copywriters, 'and it worked.'

Usually, of course, as almost every advertising man will admit, the client knows more about his product and its uses than the agency is ever going to learn (the head of merchandising at Lennen & Newell claims that he wouldn't have anybody working for him who didn't know more about the client's product than any single person in the client company; but this attitude is uncommon). What the copywriter usually contributes to the client is not so much his understanding of the product itself as his intuitive knowledge of public attitudes. His job is not to make the campaign theme logically watertight in terms of the product

36

and its features, but to convince his readers, with whatever logic or illogic best buttresses the claim, that they want what he is selling.

Technically, the task falls into two parts: catching the readers' attention and then winning their belief. Both halves of the job require, however, much the same insight into the workings of the public mind. Every agency has rules to guide copywriters and artists in their efforts to 'stop' the reader or television watcher (David Ogilvy's codex contains the bald prescription, 'to attract women, show babies or women; to attract men, show men'), but nobody contends that these rules can pull an ad any higher than the standard level of mediocrity. Research of the various kinds can help the copywriter find the arguments the public wishes to believe, but research, like rules, can do nothing to make an ad extraordinary. Only the copywriter's talent, working on the research reports as though they were part of the copywriter's own experience, can give an ad unusual effectiveness. Outside the few agencies which are strongly research-minded, like McCann-Erickson, most advertising men would rather have a copywriter ignore the research reports if the material they contain does not convince him. 'Too many copywriters,' says Ogilvy, 'are using research as a drunken man uses a lamppost—for support, rather than illumination.'

Almost every copy chief believes that the people under him spend too little time going into the market place and talking to customers. 'They don't do enough investigating of what the product is like where it's being sold,' says George Gribbin of Y & R, who started his advertising career with the May Company department store in Cleveland. 'Department store training is inadequate for agency advertising, because department store advertising is news, and it's read as news. But it has one advantage. In a store, the copywriter has to be his own reporter, his own contact man with the buyers. He doesn't have a research department to feed him information. He has to go down where the customers are to get his information by himself.'

Talking with customer, dealers, and people at the client company will often given a copywriter the necessary verisimilitudinous headline for his ad; sometimes it will even provide a slogan for an entire campaign. All the Foote, Cone headlines for the first Edsel campaign came out of eavesdropping while visitors and prospective dealers discussed the car with the Edsel sales department. 'I'd Walk a Mile for a Camel' was, if legend may be believed, said to a billboard painter by a man who had just bummed a cigarette from him. 'Ask the Man Who Owns One' appeared in a letter from the president of the Packard Company to a correspondent who had inquired about Packard's car. One of the best-remembered of all advertisements carried as its headline the astonished remark of the co-owner of a mail-order fruit business when the head of his advertising agency showed him the proposed media schedule for the next season: 'Imagine Harry and Me Advertising Our Pears in *Fortune*!'

Special problems for the copywriter may be posed by the medium in which the ad will appear. 'All women want to be beautiful,' says Howard Connell of Foote, Cone, 'and that's always the basic theme for a cosmetic. But you'd use a different appeal for a sixteen-year-old girl and a thirty-five-year-old woman; you wouldn't run the same ad in *Seventeen* and in *Vogue*.' Again, the advertisement may have to be tailored to the talents or the prejudices of a television entertainer: thus Grey Advertising, putting a commercial for Lilt on *I Love Lucy*, worked long and hard to write something which Lucille Ball and Desi Arnaz would feel was 'our kind of thing', and thereby eligible for delivery by the stars of the show themselves. Or the special interests of the audience may dictate a particular approach: Ed Zern's ads for Nash in *Field & Stream* are about hunting and fishing almost as much as they are about Nash, though they keep the same selling points that Nash uses in more general media.

Every once in a while the copywriter's feeling for believability will force an odd change in a client's marketing pattern. Foote, Cone, for example, worked up what is considered to be a particularly persuasive campaign on the excellence of Johnson's car polish and what it could do for the finish of an automobile. But the creative staff felt that nobody would believe it of a wax selling for 69 cents a jar and that people would be wary about applying a cheap wax to the paint job of their expensive automobile. Tests were run at different prices, and the higher-priced cans sold better. Johnson added some new and expensive ingredients to the polish, upped the advertising budget, and priced the product at $1.69.

3

The copywriter's talent is merely one of the many that go into the production of a finished advertisement, in print or in broadcast; but it is generally true to say that the art director, the television director, the photographer or artist, the cameraman or photoengraver, must all fit their work within the frame of the copywriter's presentation of the established campaign theme. A few individual art directors have shown themselves to be first-class salesmen, and the copywriters who work with them listen carefully to what they say—but articulate artists usually move up to be copywriters, or factota in the over-all creative department, where the pay is better. A few agencies—most notably Doyle Dane Bernbach—work on the principle that the copywriter and the artist are equal, and that an art director's inability to find a powerful visual image for a copywriter's idea is quite possibly the copywriter's fault and not the artist's. 'There was a time,' says Bernbach's Bob Gage, 'when copy people would write copy and make little sketches; they'd send in a typed sheet and some bad little drawings, and tell the art director to make layouts. But it was hollow. Here, in this shop, every art director has to be an idea man. He has to know how to think and he has to want to sell.'

As an ordinary matter, however, the approach Gage regards as dead and gone persists as normal operating procedure at other agencies, and the art director who wishes to exert influence in the final advertising can do so only by consistently and quietly making the copywriter look better than he is. Decisions about the kind of illustration to use—photographs, paintings, line drawings, cartoons—are worked out by the copywriter and the art director together, the art director proposing and the copywriter disposing (subject to further approval higher up). Usually, the art director chooses the artist or the photographer and models who will do the actual art work (except at small agencies, which live partly by extra fees for finished art, agency art directors do not paint the pictures; they do layouts, and rough sketches to guide an outside artist or a subordinate employee). But a new photographer or artist on an account must be approved by the copywriter and the account executive before the art director can give out the assignment. And at some agencies the choice of photographer or artist is in the hands of the copy chief, with the art director merely cheering from the sidelines. Kay Daly of Norman, Craig & Kummel chooses photographers and models for the ads she supervises, and goes to the photographer's studio to make sure he gets the mood she wants.

Backgrounds, clothing and accessories in the final illustration are almost as carefully watched as the sales argument itself. Most large agencies have 'styling departments', which are responsible (under the art director and, probably, the copywriter) for setting the right scene in the ad. Thus, for example, art director Harry Olsen of BBDO tells his styling department to be sure that the bowl in which the Campbell's soup will repose, the plate under the bowl, the spoon beside the plate, the table linen and the table itself are all 'a *little* above the average taste, but not all the way over into the gourmet end that would put it out of the reach of the general public'. A home economics staff bakes the cakes and cooks the meat for food advertisements; dress designers will create creations, and have them executed by costume shops or 'little dressmakers', for those ads (mostly cosmetics) which require what is called high style.

A number of technical talents go into the final print advertisement, which would be much less professional without them. Most larger agencies have a staff typographer, who picks the type face which fits best into the general 'feel' of the campaign. (It is amazing how passionately art people and typographers will argue about the relative merits of serif types—those with ornamental touches, such as little vertical lines coming down from the ends of the top bar of a T—as against the more stark sans-serif style. David Ogilvy, who employs two typographers, feels this sort of discussion is easily overdone; he likes to visualize two smartly dressed women walking down Fifth Avenue, one saying to the other, 'You know, I'd have tried that new toilet soap if only they hadn't set the body copy in nine-point Garamond.') At every agency, large or small, there is a production department or a production man who works with an outside photoengraver to make sure the art work will reproduce properly in the newspapers or magazines in which it will appear.

Copywriters and art directors often want big, black newspaper ads to help establish a 'masculine' image; but ink will smudge on a newspaper page. (This is especially so if the ad is to appear on a page which is printed on the 'first impression', when a blank roll of newsprint goes through the press, which prints one side only. The paper then twists over a roller and comes back under another press which prints the other side, or 'second impression'. The action of the roller on the still wet ink of the first impression may make a mess of any ad which tries for a solid black effect in any part of the art work. Newspapers cannot tell an agency in advance whether an ad will be printed first or second impression, so the illustration must be light enough to reproduce well either way. These problems have been multiplied by the introduction of colour printing in newspapers; 'first impression' colour ads, unless very carefully planned by production department and photoengraver, can come to look like a sloppy painter's palette rather than an illustration of a product.)

Even magazine reproduction, though infinitely better than anything a newspaper can offer (because a magazine is printed on coated paper, which fits more evenly against the printing plate than newsprint does, and does not have newsprint's ugly habit of absorbing and spreading the ink), presents grave problems to the production department. A full-colour advertisement is made up of numberless little dots, as many as 28,000 to a square inch of paper, each dot in one of only four colours (yellow, red, blue and black, printed in that order from four separate plates). Some colours—shoe-leather brown, for example—are extremely hard to reproduce from the standard four-colour palette. Even more serious are manufacturers' off-colour packages, which, everyone feels, should appear in print in precisely the right hue. Where the company is a big enough advertiser, the magazines may be extra co-operative: thus Campbell's Soup—which has had the premier position in the *Saturday Evening Post* since the memory of man runneth not to the contrary (the position is the first ad after the central reading section)—has arranged with *Life* and the *Post* for a separate red ink, the colour of the Campbell's package, in the printing of Campbell's ads.

When artist and copywriter wish to achieve subtle effects, shading pastels and a romantic mood, they are often licked by the high speeds at which magazines print their issues. Subtle colour effects are produced by the adjacency of the little colour dots (which do not print one on top of the other, but side by side, as examination of a colour advertisement through a good magnifying glass will quickly demonstrate). For the effect in the original colour photograph to be reproduced exactly, there cannot be so much as a millimetre of tolerance in the angle and position of the four separate printing plates: each one must strike the page at precisely the same point. The mass circulation magazines, printing five and six million copies a week, use presses which turn out upwards of seven hundred copies a minute, and at such speeds precise 'registration' is impossible. Every once in a while the registration goes off completely (double lines around the automobile, or the shadow of a second pair of lips on the girl's chin), in which case the agency may ask, and may receive, a cash rebate from the magazine, or a 'make-good', a rerun of the advertisement at no charge. ('You never,' says production director Eli Gordon of Thompson, somewhat grimly, 'get a make-good from *Life* or the *Post*.') But the registration may be off so slightly that the naked eye cannot see anything wrong with the picture—and yet the saddened production man and the miserable art director note the muddy ruination by inexact registration of a delicate piece of art work, lovingly hand-finished at the photoengraver's by a retoucher who is an artist himself ('And why shouldn't he be?' argues Grey's Ralph Froelich, 'why should he ruin a good Ektachrome by rubbing down the eyebrows when they ought to be bold?'), proved on the magazine's own paper stock by the photoengraver's own high-speed press, guaranteed to the client as perfect ... There is nothing to be done about it, just as there is nothing to be done when the picture of an elephant's backside, printed on the other side of the page, strikes through the pale Bahama waters of the bathing-suit advertisement, placing the bathing beauty in a position as uncomfortable as it is unglamorous. Nobody knows what an advertising man suffers.

4

For television advertising all the rules are different. The campaign theme must be visualized not as an illustration but in terms of what Rosser Reeves calls the 'video gimmick' (he used to call it the 'video device', but shorthand at Bates reduced this phrase to VD, which he felt gave the agency an unhealthy look). The creative reference frame is not prose composition ('I don't think,' says George Gribbin, 'that a television copywriter particularly needs a feeling for words'), but dramatic timing. Excellent print copywriters with a gift for static illustration, who had no trouble tossing off forensics for radio announcers, found themselves unmanned by the combination of moving pictures and spoken words. Often they lack even the most elementary sense of timing: 'You'll get instructions,' says Rex Cox of Sarra, one of the half dozen largest producers of television film commercials, 'which tell you to show a man coming home, kissing his wife, sitting down in the easy chair, putting on his slippers, reaching for a glass of beer—and that's going to take eighteen seconds, even at a dead run—and on the audio side, all the announcer has to say is, "Always reach for So-and-so's beer." Or it will go the other way; the screen is just supposed to show a man reaching out his hand for a glass of beer, while the audio has a long spiel for the product.'

At the beginning the agencies generally handled this problem by turning over to firms like Sarra and Transfilm a set of rough ideas for a script, which the television film company was to 'work up' into a commercial. Meanwhile, the agencies beat the bushes for new personnel, impressing recruits from the drama schools and the ranks of unperformed playwrights, and forming them together in rough marching order as a 'television copy department'. This experiment in the managing of a new form turned out not to be entirely successful, partly because it produced different approaches for television and print copy, vitiating the strength of the campaign theme, and partly because the dragooned playwrights often had little instinct for selling.

The next step at some agencies (especially those which concentrate on broadcast commercials, like Ted Bates and William Esty) was to consolidate the two copy departments, with television work channelled to the more salesmanlike of the new talents and the more dramatically facile of the old copywriters. At others, the separate television department was maintained, but with television copywriters firmly slotted under the thumb of the group head, a print copy man. A few of the largest agencies absorbed their new television writers into over-all television departments, which worked on programmes as well as commercials; and a man from the television department was slipped into each creative group, to act as technical counsel to and occasional substitute for the copywriter who wrote the print advertising. Thus, the wheel turned full circle, and the print copywriter, as the experienced planner of approaches to the sales argument, became once again the man who decided whether the TV commercial should show 'real' people or prominent personalities or cartoon characters or the product itself in motion (like the marching Lucky Strike cigarettes which provided an opening for *Your Hit Parade* for more than six years). But now the print copywriters knows—or can easily find out—what he is doing.

What goes to the television film company these days is a complete shooting script, plus a 'story board', a set of rough drawings placed in television-screen-shaped boxes, which are to guide the film director in putting together the commercial (or the television director if the commercial is to be broadcast 'live'). Usually the script is submitted to several companies—there are dozens of them now, including all the major Hollywood studios— and bids are solicited for the job. (Cartoons cost more than commercials which use live action, but they can probably be shown more often before the audience gets sick of them.) Over to the television film studio when the deal has been made traipse the agency's stylists and home economists, casting experts and a director from the agency's television department, and the copywriter, who must be present to change lines if it appears that an actor is uncomfortable with the script, or that the sound track runs 62 seconds instead of the required 58 seconds. In the text-books it says that 125 words a minute will do just about right, but the copywriter cannot be sure his script will come out on the button until he sees an actor read it in synchronization with the relevant pictures. Getting everything to come out exactly on time—60 seconds of picture, 58 seconds of sound—is the simple, nagging problem that takes all the time in the studio.

In and around the shooting stage, usually a room two stories high, hung with Klieg lights and microphone booms and cameras on infinitely adjustable pedestals, stand the actors and actresses, half a dozen people from the agency, the film company's own producer and director, two cameramen, a sound engineer, assorted stagehands and lighting engineers, and perhaps even somebody from the client's advertising department. This great assemblage of expertise watches and coaches and makes suggestions, and finally it all goes perfectly—except that it's $1\frac{1}{2}$ seconds too long, in a place that the film editor won't be able to cut. So everything starts over again; Hollywood figures five 'takes' for every finished scene, but a television commercial demands ten. In advertising, it's always what looks easiest, and least-worth-doing-anyway, that causes the most anguish.

44

SECTION II Broadcasting: the Nature and Exploitation of Radio and Television

No one disputes the vast importance of radio and television in the contemporary world, but the exact nature of these media and the extent of their effects remains a puzzle. This section brings together some important documents in the debate which has raged, and will rage, for years though it is now largely concentrated on TV. Broadly, there are three areas that invite coverage. As a convenience of analysis I shall separate them here, though they obviously interact at all points. The first is the nature of the media of broadcasting; second, the situation in British TV; third, the ascertainable effects of TV upon the public.

(i) The nature of the media: general

The primary fact about broadcasting is that it is accessible to a very large number of people, virtually the entire population. Of its nature, then, broadcasting must seek common denominators in this mass audience. I do not use the term 'lowest' common denominator, but broadcasting is inherently vulnerable to the charge that in aiming at mass appeal it lowers standards of programme content and presentation. This charge has frequently been voiced. Thus, Philip Abrams, in his critical analysis of the tendencies inherent in broadcasting,[1] identifies trivialization,

[1] Philip Abrams, 'Radio and television'. *Discrimination and Popular Culture,* ed. Denys Thompson (Penguin, 1964), pp. 50–66.

45

universality (the concept of a mass audience, rather than a number of smaller audiences), continuity, and domesticity as the forces that perennially affect radio and TV. Again, R. H. S. Crossman, in his dispassionate survey of TV and politics,[1] *found it necessary to refer to the 'trivialization' and 'sensationalism' of TV coverage in that field. Broadcasting, clearly, has to live with a recurring concern about the way in which its tendencies have developed. But the specific title of Mr Crossman's address indicates that it is now, more than in the past, necessary to draw distinctions between the two media of broadcasting. Our consciousness of these distinctions has grown rapidly of late years. As recently as 1964, it was possible for Mr. Abrams to treat together of radio and TV for the purpose of general coverage. Nowadays one qualifies very markedly generalizations that bring radio and TV together, or which assume that TV is radio plus vision. Our awareness of the different natures of radio and TV is due in considerable part to the writings of Marshall McLuhan. Of recent years he has been the centre of a furious critical controversy, one rendered all the more inflamed by the brute fact that our present state of communications research does not enable us to make an adequate critique of McLuhan's writings (of which the most important are* The Gutenberg Galaxy, *1962, and* Understanding Media, *1964). McLuhan is a seminal thinker whose achievement is to initiate a fundamental scrutiny of the nature of all media. He holds that it is nonsense to make a simple distinction between 'form' and 'content', one which assumes that 'form' is a neutral medium for canalizing a definite and pre-existent 'content'. On the contrary: the form (or medium) dominates the content; 'the medium is the message'. This is the central McLuhan position. From it, he investigates all contemporary media, using in all cases a basic tool for analysis, the distinction between 'hot' and 'cold' media. 'Hot' media extend one sense-mode with high-definition data; examples are the film and radio. 'Cold' media provide low-definition data, requiring much more participation by the individual; examples are the television, telephone, and cartoon. All this is highly controversial. The reader coming*

[1] R. H. S. Crossman, 'Politics and Television'. Granada Lecture, October 21st, 1968.

fresh to McLuhan will find him a difficult, but immensely rewarding guide to the media. His ideas, allege his critics, have never been clearly formulated; for example, the 'hot-cold' metaphor runs speedily into difficulties (is the living theatre significantly different in the front and rear stalls?). But no student of communications can afford to neglect the immense challenge of McLuhan's ideas.[1]

It is clear that some of Mr Abrams' generalizations about broadcasting call for re-assessment today. The role of radio is diverging from that of TV. A generation ago, a radio set was a large and seldom-moved piece of furniture, the centrepiece of the family living-room, and the major focus of national entertainment. Now radio has become cheap, portable, and private. Many young people own a transistor radio; and radio has abandoned its former role to TV. The programming of radio reflects this, and demonstrates that radio is resisting the tendencies to universality. For the great point about radio today is that it concentrates on small audiences, not a single mass audience. Broadly, there are two sorts of small audience; special interest, and local. The strategy of radio broadcasting today is that an individual listener should have the maximum opportunity to indulge his private tastes (pop music, drama, beginner's German), and to that end the four main BBC channels each have clearly-defined characters and functions. (The details of this policy are controversial, but the general strategy is clear.) The expansion of local broadcasting in the seventies will extend this principle. Whether it supplies background music or programmes requiring some concentration, radio is above all directed to the private individual.

TV-viewing, obviously, is much more a group affair. People watch it in groups; the programmes are shaped with a very wide range of audience in mind. The fact is that whatever the inherent dissimilarities between the effects of radio and TV, their organization and operation proceed on quite different principles. In Britain, TV broadcasting is in essence a struggle between two institutions, the BBC and ITA, for the same audience. Each institution holds, with some fluctuation, about 50 per cent of

[1] The debate can conveniently be pursued in *McLuhan Hot and Cold*, ed. G. E. Stearn, Penguin, 1968.

47

that audience; neither institution is able to stray far from the TAM ratings. Radio, on the contrary, is essentially a single organization (BBC) operating on a large number of wavelengths. It therefore thinks in terms of satisfying many small audiences, since it has no need to compete for a mass audience. Thus the problematical distinctions between the basic properties of the two media are accentuated, and perhaps confused, by the different character *of radio and TV as organized at present in Britain.*

(*ii*) The purposes of broadcasting, and the performances of BBC and ITA

We now turn specifically to television and the situation obtaining in Britain under the two broadcasting authorities, BBC and ITA. This situation has been examined most notably in the formidable report prepared by the Royal Commission on Broadcasting submitted in 1962. The Commission, under the Chairmanship of Sir Harry Pilkington, has put on record an exhaustive discussion of the principles and methods appropriate to public broadcasting. As a statistical survey, the report is already somewhat out of date. As an exposition of the underlying debate, it will remain relevant for many years; and I have quoted extensively from this document.

The Pilkington Report raises the simple and basic question: does TV possess considerable power to influence its audience? The Commission put this question to the BBC and ITA. BBC answered in the affirmative, and accepted the corollary, that it was their duty to ensure a high standard of programming for the public. ITA, on the other hand, thought not; it was their view that the public selected programmes to suit their tastes, rather than were influenced by programmes. They could, therefore, see no harm in a television service whose great principle was entertainment for a mass audience. Here is a clear-cut conflict of view, and the Commission threw its weight entirely on to the side of the BBC. It cited the considerable dissatisfaction with the quality of programmes provided by the ITA, and laid down the principle that (in the absence of decisive research demonstrations to the contrary) it must be the working assumption that TV has considerable power to influence values and moral standards. The

Report recommended that there should be certain structural changes in the ITA, and that the forthcoming third channel should be awarded to the BBC.

The Report had a lively public reception. The supporters of Independent Television branded it as a neo-Puritan assault upon the people's pleasures; the opponents embraced it as a reform scarcely paralleled since the casting-out of the money-changers from the Temple. A number of scholars in the middle, of no determinate moral orientation, expressed grave doubts on the validity of the Report's central assumption, concerning the effects of TV. (See, for example, J. A. C. Brown's Techniques of Persuasion, *Penguin, 1963.) Nevertheless, the case made out in the Report was largely accepted by the Government of the day. The central body in Independent Television, the ITA, was strengthened vis-à-vis the Companies, and the coveted third channel awarded to the BBC (BBC-2). Now that the controversy following the Report's publication has died down, it is possible to see it as a warning shot fired across the bows of commercial TV. For ITV has undoubtedly mended its ways noticeably since the Pilkington Report. The production of serious programmes on ITV has increased from 19 per cent in 1956 to 40 per cent in 1966.[1] Moreover, the contracts of the Independent Television Companies are reviewed every ten years. The experience of the unlucky TWW—whose licence to operate was not renewed in 1967—has served notice that the backmarkers of the Companies have no prescriptive right to exist. The Pilkington Report has beyond question had a powerful and enduring effect on the development of British broadcasting.*

It is instructive to note the situation, which offers certain parallels, now developing in American TV. The situation there is now hard to assess, as an important transitional stage has arisen. The dominance of TV in the United States by the giant commercial networks (NBC, CBS, and ABC) has for years met with public criticism, and in 1967 two major proposals signalled an important challenge to commercial TV. The Carnegie Commission, whose aims were endorsed by President Johnson, recommended that a Public Broadcasting Corporation be set up,

[1] See Joseph Weltman, 'The Present Pattern in Television and Radio', in *Educational Television and Radio in Britain*, BBC (1966), p. 71.

free of Government control, and dedicated to the production of quality programmes. Very broadly, the Ford Foundation's proposals pointed the same way. But their conceptions of this Public Broadcasting service differed sharply. Carnegie saw it as based on a regional and local service, rather than a fourth national network. It would be financed principally by a manufacturer's excise on TV sets. Ford, in contrast, envisaged a national network based on a satellite system. As between these two proposals, the Public Television Act of 1967 (it became law on November 7th) made no decisive choice. The issues of localism versus the network, of connection by satellite versus connection by land-lines, and of the sources of financing, are still undecided. Nevertheless, a start has been made. Government support for the concept of Public Broadcasting is now established and a foundation on which to build is created. Experimental broadcasting, for two hours each Sunday night, known as PBL (Public Broadcasting Laboratory), began in November, 1967.

(*iii*) The effects of TV upon the public

This is one of the critical areas of communications study. It is not even easy to formulate the problem satisfactorily. Clearly, watching TV is an experience that (like all experiences) must affect our future behaviour. But how? The old idea, very simple and brutally unsophisticated, went something like this: one watched acts of violence (say) on TV; one went out of the house and did likewise. Similarly with acts of sex, anti-social behaviour, and so on. To which a very obvious counter-theory applies; watching TV is purgative, or therapeutic. It is a matter of common observation that anyone who has watched a boxing match on TV is in no fit state afterwards to carry out any aggressive action. The theories cancel out; what of the evidence? So far the sociologists have had no positive results from the crucial correlation that must be established, that between watching acts of violence on TV, and performing actual crimes afterwards. This does not mean that no such correlation exists, only that research has so far proved negative. So the old crude theory of TV's effects has turned out to be not very useful. A great deal of research, however, has been put into communications-effects,[1] *and there is no question that TV exercises a subtle, complex, and important role in people's lives. But that role will not yield to simple cause-effects formulations.*

I have selected certain documents that throw some light on the media-audience relationhips. The first things we need to know are what *people watch, and in what numbers. Reasonably satisfactory answers to this are given by the audience-measurement techniques, and I reproduce ITA's account of the measurement system they employ. This is based on household viewing, while the BBC's is based on individual interviews; consequently the statistics advanced by the two organizations differ somewhat. But there is no reason to doubt the approximate accuracy of the figures, and the table included here shows what the British public was actually viewing in a given week of September, 1969. The effects of broadcasting on children have been the subject of major pioneer research of recent years, most importantly by the teams led by Hilde T. Himmelweit, in Britain, and Wilbur Schramm, in the USA and Canada. In spite of the differences between England and North America, and in the methodological approach, these two studies* (Television and the Child (O.U.P.) 1958; Television in the Lives of our Children, 1961) *provide a general correspondence of results, when they can be compared. The methods of research employed demand a brief description. The Himmelweit survey studied the lives of several thousand school-children, in four English cities, on a very careful comparative basis. The children were divided into two major groups, with and without a TV set in the homes; and they were 'twinned' by age, sex, I.Q., and parental income group. Thus the working hypothesis of the research was that the children were 'equal' in the four important categories, but 'unequal' in that one group was exposed to TV, the other not. Differences in the habits, behaviour, and school progress of the children could thus be checked. The American survey adopted several methods, but made a special study of two neighbouring Canadian towns, one*

[1] See, for example, Joseph T. Klapper, *The Effects of Mass Communication* (Illinois: The Free Press of Glencoe), 1960; and Paul F. Lazarsfeld and Robert K. Merton, 'Mass Communication, Popular Taste, and Organized Social Action', in *Mass Communications*, ed. Wilbur Schramm (Urbana: University of Illinois), 1960, pp. 492–512.

with no community TV available (Radiotown) and one with (Teletown).

The once widespread idea that TV encourages passivity is investigated by Himmelweit, and the major finding is that in none of the five senses of the term does TV encourage passivity. (McLuhan regards TV as a highly involving medium, demanding strong participation.) Violence on TV is always a matter of great concern, and here the Himmelweit survey affords a precise approach. The distinction between 'stylized' and 'realistic' violence is essential, and its effect in inducing fear and anxiety in children is very thoroughly analysed.

Schramm, in his analysis of TV programmes, employs a classification of fundamental importance. He distinguishes between fantasy *and* reality. *Fantasy programmes turn their backs on the real world and offer entertainment and escape, while reality programmes involve the viewer in real-life situations and problems and offer enlightenment. The two categories are not incompatible, and many programmes combine them. But in general Westerns, pop shows, and crime thrillers belong to the domain of fantasy, documentaries and news to that of reality. The danger Schramm discerns is that the child may fail to identify the frontier between reality and fantasy—he may cross and re-cross that frontier several times in an evening. The picture the child obtains of the 'real' world may not be an accurate and balanced one; the world as portrayed is composed of the imbecile parent of the situation comedy, the easy sex, the* neutral *attitude to violence of the thriller. In sum, the theory advanced by Schramm is that the child 'is absorbing a markedly erroneous picture of adult life', and that it may make later adjustment difficult. This is a much more subtle version of the theory that the staple fare of TV has an adverse effect, on a young audience especially. The matter is put thus in the latest report from Leicester University's Television Research Committee: 'There is sufficient evidence to suggest that television affects adolescent life-styles and aspirations.'[1] These tentative formulations of an effect-theory serve to remind us of the difficulties of theorizing in this field, and the difficulties of demonstration. To*

[1] Television Research Committee, *Second Progress Report and Recommendations* (Leicester University Press, 1969), p. 31.

relate the 'world-picture' derived from TV by a child, to its social adjustment in adult life, is a virtually impossible task. Yet all our hypotheses must start from the assumption that such a relationship exists.

The argument of Professor Schramm is that the effect of TV may be to blur the distinction between fantasy and reality. Julian Critchley, TV critic for The Times, goes further: he asserts that TV distorts reality itself, and that the selectivity of TV news provides its own form of misrepresentation. This is a central assault on TV that not all will agree with; but it is the view of a distinguished critic of the medium, and deserves to be weighed with respect. I cite Mr Critchley as a representative of a profoundly important trend: the old, crude ideas of the evils of TV are now giving way to vastly more sophisticated, intelligent and well-informed doubts.

To conclude, there is the question of TV's role for the community as a whole—that is, not simply limited audiences of children, adults, special-interest groups, but the entire viewing population. On great occasions TV has a unique faculty of focusing the thoughts and emotions of the entire viewing population. McLuhan's idea of the globe as an 'electronic village' is very far, as yet, from being realized; but it is perfectly possible for a literal majority of an entire country—men, women, and children—to be an audience, or congregation, that participates simultaneously in a central national event. To such great occasions—for example, the funeral of Sir Winston Churchill, or the final of the 1966 World Cup between England and Germany—a profound symbolic significance is attached. In the USA, much the best example of recent years is the assassination of President Kennedy. Ruth Leeds Love's study of the television coverage is particularly fascinating on the detailed problems of taste, or situational appropriateness, with which producers were faced. For the community to participate at the desired level, such matters are all-important. On the greatest of national occasions, universality—far from meriting criticism—is the only acceptable principle of public communication.

7 Number of radio and television sets per 1000 population in select countries 1968

	Radio receivers	Television sets
Australia	⬜=⬜=[	⬜⬜
Austria	⬜=⬜=⬜=	⬜[
Argentine	⬜=⬜=⬜=[	⬜
Canada	⬜=⬜=⬜=⬜=⬜=⬜=	⬜⬜⬜
Columbia	⬜=[	[
France	⬜=⬜=⬜=[	⬜⬜
India	⬜=⬜	
Italy	⬜=⬜=⬜=⬜=⬜=⬜=⬜=⬜=⬜=	⬜
U.S.A.	⬜=⬜=⬜=⬜=⬜=⬜=⬜=⬜=⬜=⬜=⬜=⬜=⬜=⬜=	⬜⬜⬜⬜
Japan	⬜=⬜=⬜	⬜⬜
Mexico	⬜=⬜=[	[
Netherlands	⬜=⬜=[	⬜⬜
Nigeria	⬜=[	
Sweden	⬜=⬜=⬜=⬜=	⬜⬜⬜
Turkey	⬜=	
U.K.	⬜=⬜=⬜=[	⬜⬜⬜
U.S.S.R.	⬜=⬜=⬜=[	⬜

Radio receivers scale: 0, 100, 200, 300, 400, 500, 600, 700, 800, 900, 1000, 1100, 1200, 1300, 1400

Television sets scale: 0, 100, 200, 300, 400

Number per 1000 population

Source: U.N. Statistical Yearbook 1968

8　From: Understanding Media by Marshall McLuhan

Radio

The Tribal Drum

England and America had had their 'shots' against radio in the form of long exposure to literacy and industrialism. These forms involve an intense visual organization of experience. The more earthy and less visual European cultures were not immune to radio. Its tribal magic was not lost on them, and the old web of kinship began to resonate once more with the note of fascism. The inability of literate people to grasp the language and message of the media as such is involuntarily conveyed by the comments of sociologist Paul Lazarsfeld in discussing the effects of radio:

> The last group of effects may be called the monopolistic effects of radio. Such have attracted most public attention because of their importance in the totalitarian countries. If a government monopolizes the radio, then by mere repetition and by exclusion of conflicting points of view it can determine the opinions of the population. We do not know much about how this monopolistic effect really works, but it is important to note its singularity. No inference should be drawn regarding the effects of radio as such. It is often forgotten that Hitler did not achieve control through radio but almost despite it, because at the time of his rise to power radio was controlled by his enemies. The monopolistic effects have probably less social importance than is generally assumed.

Professor Lazarsfeld's helpless unawareness of the nature and effects of radio is not a personal defect, but a universally shared ineptitude.

In a radio speech in Munich, March 14, 1936, Hitler said, 'I go my way with the assurance of a somnambulist.' His victims and his critics have been equally somnambulistic. They danced entranced to the tribal drum of radio that extended their central nervous system to create depth involvement for everybody. 'I live right inside radio when I listen. I more easily lose myself in radio than in a book,' said a voice from a radio poll. The power of radio to involve people in depth is manifested in its use during homework by youngsters and by many other people who carry transistor sets in order to provide a private world for themselves amidst crowds. There is a little poem by the German dramatist Bertholt Brecht:

> You little box, held to me when escaping
> So that your valves should not break,
> Carried from house to ship from ship to train,
> So that my enemies might go on talking to me
> Near my bed, to my pain
> The last thing at night, the first thing in the morning,
> Of their victories and of my cares,
> Promise me not to go silent all of a sudden.

One of the many effects of television on radio has been to shift radio from an entertainment medium into a kind of nervous information system. News bulletins, time signals, traffic data, and, above all, weather reports now serve to enhance the native power of radio to involve people in one another. Weather is that medium that involves all people equally. It is the top item on radio, showering us with fountains of auditory space or *lebensraum*.

It was no accident that Senator McCarthy lasted such a very short time when he switched to TV. Soon the press decided, 'He isn't news any more.' Neither McCarthy nor the press ever knew what had happened. TV is a cool medium. It rejects hot figures and hot issues and people from the hot press media. Fred Allen was a casualty of TV. Was Marilyn Monroe? Had TV occurred on a large scale during Hitler's reign he would have vanished quickly. Had TV come first there would have been no Hitler at all. When Khrushchev appeared on American TV he was more acceptable than Nixon, as a clown and a lovable sort of old boy. His appearance is rendered by TV as a comic cartoon. Radio, however, is a hot medium and takes cartoon characters seriously. Mr K. on radio would be a different proposition.

In the Kennedy-Nixon debates, those who heard them on radio received an overwhelming idea of Nixon's superiority. It was Nixon's fate to provide a sharp, high-definition image and action for the cool TV medium that translated that sharp image into the impression of a phony. I suppose 'phony' is something that resonates wrong, that doesn't *ring* true. It might well be that F.D.R.

would not have done well on TV. He had learned, at least, how to use the hot radio medium for his very cool job of fireside chatting. He first, however, had had to hot up the press media against himself in order to create the right atmosphere for his radio chats. He learned how to use the press in close relation to radio. TV would have presented him with an entirely different political and social mix of components and problems. He would possibly have enjoyed solving them, for he had the kind of playful approach necessary for tackling new and obscure relationships.

Radio affects most people intimately, person-to-person, offering a world of unspoken communication between writer-speaker and the listener. That is the immediate aspect of radio. A private experience. The subliminal depths of radio are charged with the resonating echoes of tribal horns and antique drums. This is inherent in the very nature of this medium, with its power to turn the psyche and society into a single echo chamber. The resonating dimension of radio is unheeded by the script writers, with few exceptions. The famous Orson Welles broadcast about the invasion from Mars was a simple demonstration of the all-inclusive completely involving scope of the auditory image of radio. It was Hitler who gave radio the Orson Welles treatment for *real*.

That Hitler came into political existence at all is directly owing to radio and public-address systems. This is not to say that these media relayed his thoughts effectively to the German people. His thoughts were of very little consequence. Radio provided the first massive experience of electronic implosion, that reversal of the entire direction and meaning of literate Western civilization. For tribal peoples, for those whose entire social existence is an extension of family life, radio will continue to be a violent experience. Highly literate societies, that have long subordinated family life to individualist stress in business and politics, have managed to absorb and to neutralize the radio implosion without revolution. Not so, those communities that have had only brief or superficial experience of literacy. For them, radio is utterly explosive.

To understand such effects, it is necessary to see literacy as typographic technology, applied not only to the rationalizing of the entire procedures of production and marketing, but to law and education and city planning, as well. The principles of continuity, uniformity, and repeatability derived from print technology have, in England and America, long permeated every phase of communal life. In those areas a child learns literacy from traffic and street, from every car and toy and garment. Learning to read and write is a minor facet of literacy in the uniform, continuous environments of the English-speaking world. Stress on literacy is a distinguishing mark of areas that are striving to initiate that process of standardization that leads to the visual organization of work and space. Without psychic transformation of the inner life into segmented visual terms by literacy, there cannot be the economic 'take-off' that insures a continual movement of augmented production and perpetually accelerated change-and-exchange of goods and services.

Just prior to 1914, the Germans had become obsessed with the menace of 'encirclement'. Their neighbours had all developed elaborate railway systems that facilitated mobilization of manpower resources. Encirclement is a highly visual image that had great novelty for this newly industrialized nation. In the 1930s, by contrast, the German obsession was with *lebensraum*. This is not a visual concern, at all. It is a claustrophobia, engendered by the radio implosion and compression of space. The German defeat had thrust them back from visual obsession into brooding upon the resonating Africa within. The tribal past has never ceased to be a reality for the German psyche.

It was the ready access of the German and middle-European world to the rich nonvisual resources of auditory and tactile form that enabled them to enrich the world of music and dance and sculpture. Above all their tribal mode gave them easy access to the new nonvisual world of subatomic physics, in which long-literate and long-industrialized societies are decidedly handicapped. The rich area of preliterate vitality felt the hot impact of radio. The message of radio is one of violent, unified implosion and resonance. For Africa, India, China, and even Russia, radio is a profound archaic force, a time bond with the most ancient past and long-forgotten experience.

Tradition, in a word, is the sense of the total past as *now*. Its awakening is a natural result of radio impact and of electric information, in general. For the intensely literate population, however, radio engendered a profound unlocalizable sense of guilt that sometimes expressed itself in the fellow-traveller attitude. A newly found human involvement bred anxiety and insecurity and unpredictability. Since literacy had fostered an extreme of individualism, and radio had done just the opposite in reviving the ancient experience of kinship webs of deep tribal involvement, the literate West tried to find some sort of compromise in a larger sense of collective responsibility. The sudden impulse to this end was just as subliminal and obscure as the earlier literary pressure toward individual isolation and irresponsibility; therefore, nobody was happy about any of the positions arrived at. The Gutenberg technology had produced a new kind of visual, national entity in the sixteenth century that was gradually meshed with industrial production and expansion. Telegraph and radio neutralized nationalism but evoked archaic tribal ghosts of the most vigorous brand. This is exactly the meeting of eye and ear, of explosion and implosion, or as Joyce puts it in the *Wake*, 'In that european end meets Ind.' The opening of the European ear brought to an end the open society and reintroduced that Indic world of tribal man to West End woman. Joyce puts these matters not so much in cryptic, as in dramatic and mimetic, form. The reader has only to take any of his phrases such as this one, and mime it until it yields the intelligible. Not a long or tedious process, if approached in the spirit of artistic playfulness that guarantees 'lots of fun at Finnegan's wake'.

Radio is provided with its cloak of invisibility, like any other medium. It comes to us ostensibly with person-to-person directness that is private and intimate, while in more urgent fact, it is really a subliminal echo chamber of magical power to touch remote and forgotten chords. All technological extensions of ourselves must be numb and subliminal, else we could not endure the leverage exerted upon us by such extension. Even more than telephone or telegraph, radio is that extension of the central nervous system that is matched only by human speech itself. Is it not worthy of our meditation that radio should be specially attuned to that primitive extension of our central nervous system, that aboriginal mass medium, the vernacular tongue? The crossing of these two most intimate and potent of human technologies could not possibly have failed to provide some extraordinary new shapes for human experience. So it proved with Hitler, the somnambulist. But does the detribalized and literate West imagine that it has earned immunity to the tribal magic of radio as a permanent possession? Our teenagers in the 1950s began to manifest many of the tribal stigmata. The adolescent, as opposed to the teenager, can now be classified as a phenomenon of literacy. Is it not significant that the adolescent was indigenous only to those areas of England and America where literacy had invested even food with abstract visual values? Europe never had adolescents. It had chaperones. Now, to the teenager, radio gives privacy, and at the same time it provides the tight tribal bond of the world of the common market, of song, and of resonance. The ear is hyperesthetic compared to the neutral eye. The ear is intolerant, closed, and exclusive, whereas the eye is open, neutral, and associative. Ideas of tolerance came to the West only after two or three centuries of literacy and visual Gutenberg culture. No such saturation with visual values had occurred in Germany by 1930. Russia is still far from any such involvement with visual order and values.

If we sit and talk in a dark room, words suddenly acquire new meanings and different textures. They become richer, even, than architecture, which Le Corbusier rightly says can best be felt at night. All those gestural qualities that the printed page strips from language come back in the dark, and on the radio. Given only the *sound* of a play, we have to fill in *all* of the senses, not just the sight of the action. So much do-it-yourself, or completion and 'closure' of action, develops a kind of independent isolation in the young that makes them remote and inaccessible. The mystic screen of sound with which they are invested by their radios provides the privacy for their homework, and immunity from parental behest.

With radio came great changes to the press, to advertising, to drama, and to poetry. Radio offered new scope to practical jokers like Morton Downey at CBS. A sportscaster had just begun his fifteen-minute reading from a script when he was joined by Mr Downey, who proceeded to remove his shoes and socks. Next followed coat and trousers and then underwear, while the sportscaster helplessly continued his broadcast, testifying to the compelling power of the mike to command loyalty over modesty and self-protective impulse.

Radio created the disk jockey, and elevated the gag writer into a major national role. Since the advent of radio, the gag has supplanted the joke, not because of gag writers, but because radio is a fast hot medium that has also rationed the reporter's space for stories.

Jean Shepherd of WOR in New York regards radio as a new medium for a new kind of novel that he writes nightly. The mike is his pen and paper. His audience and their knowledge of the daily events of the world provide his characters, his scenes, and moods. It is his idea that, just as Montaigne was the first to use the page to record his reactions to the new world of printed books, he is the first to use radio as an essay and novel form for recording our common awareness of a totally new world of universal human participation in all human events, private or collective.

To the student of media, it is difficult to explain the human indifference to social effects of these radical forces. The phonetic alphabet and the printed word that exploded the closed tribal world into the open society of fragmented functions and specialist knowledge and action have never been studied in their roles as a magical transformer. The antithetic electric power of instant information that reverses social explosion into implosion, private enterprise into organization man, and expanding empires into common markets, has obtained as little recognition as the written word. The power of radio to retribalize mankind, its almost instant reversal of individualism into collectivism, Fascist or Marxist, has gone unnoticed. So extraordinary is this unawareness that *it* is what needs to be explained. The transforming power of media is easy to explain, but the ignoring of this power is not at all easy to explain. It goes without saying that the universal ignoring of the psychic action of technology bespeaks some inherent function, some essential numbing of consciousness such as occurs under stress and shock conditions.

The history of radio is instructive as an indicator of the bias and blindness induced in any society by its pre-existent technology. The word 'wireless', still used for radio in Britain, manifests the negative 'horseless-carriage' attitude toward a new form. Early wireless was regarded as a form of telegraph, and was not seen even in relation to the telephone. David Sarnoff in 1916 sent a memo to the Director of the American Marconi Company that employed him, advocating the idea of a music box in the home. It was ignored. That was the year of the Irish Easter rebellion and of the first radio *broadcast*. Wireless had already been used on ships as ship-to-shore 'telegraph'. The Irish rebels used a ship's wireless to make, not a point-to-point message, but a diffused broadcast in the hope of getting word to some ship that would relay their story to the American press. And so it proved. Even after broadcasting had been in existence for some years, there was no commercial interest in it. It was the amateur operators or hams and their fans, whose petitions finally got some action in favour of the setting up of facilities. There was reluctance and opposition from the world of the press, which, in England, led to the formation of the BBC and the firm shackling of radio by newspaper and advertising interests. This is an obvious rivalry that has not been openly discussed. The restrictive pressure by the press on radio and TV is still a hot issue in Britain and in Canada. But, typically, misunderstanding of the nature of the medium rendered the restraining policies quite futile. Such has always been the case, most notoriously in government censorship of the press and of the movies. Although the medium is the *message*, the controls go beyond programming. The restraints are always

61

directed to the 'content', which is always another medium. The content of the press is literary statement, as the content of the book is speech, and the content of the movie is the novel. So the effects of radio are quite independent of its programming. To those who have never studied media, this fact is quite as baffling as literacy is to natives, who say, 'Why do you write? Can't you remember?'

Thus, the commercial interests who think to render media universally acceptable, invariably settle for 'entertainment' as a strategy of neutrality. A more spectacular mode of the ostrich-head-in-sand could not be devised, for it ensures maximal pervasiveness for any medium whatever. The literate community will always argue for a controversial or point-of-view use of press, radio, and movie that would in effect diminish the operation, not only of press, radio and movie, but of the book as well. The commercial entertainment strategy automatically ensures maximum speed and force of impact for any medium, on psychic and social life equally. It thus becomes a comic strategy of unwitting self-liquidation, conducted by those who are dedicated to permanence, rather than to change. In the future, the only effective media controls must take the thermostatic form of quantitative rationing. Just as we now try to control atom-bomb fallout, so we will one day try to control media fallout. Education will become recognized as civil defence against media fallout. The only medium for which our education now offers some civil defence is the print medium. The educational establishment, founded on print, does not yet admit any other responsibilities.

Radio provides a speed-up of information that also causes acceleration in other media. It certainly contracts the world to village size, and creates insatiable village tastes for gossip, rumour, and personal malice. But while radio contracts the world to village dimensions, it hasn't the effect of homogenizing the village quarters. Quite the contrary. In India, where radio is the supreme form of communication, there are more than a dozen official languages and the same number of official radio networks. The effect of radio as a reviver of archaism and ancient memories is not limited to Hitler's Germany. Ireland, Scotland, and Wales have undergone resurgence of their ancient tongues since the coming of radio, and the Israeli present an even more extreme instance of linguistic revival. They now speak a language which has been dead in books for centuries. Radio is not only a mighty awakener of archaic memories, forces, and animosities, but a decentralizing, pluralistic force, as is really the case with all electric power and media.

Centralism of organization is based on the continuous, visual, lineal structuring that arises from phonetic literacy. At first, therefore, electric media merely followed the established patterns of literate structures. Radio was released from these centralist network pressures by TV. TV then took up the burden of centralism, from which it may be released by Telstar. With TV accepting the central network burden derived from our centralized industrial organization, radio was free to diversify, and to begin a regional and local community service that it had not known, even in the earliest days of the radio 'hams'. Since TV, radio has turned to the individual needs of people at different times of the day, a fact that goes with the multiplicity of receiving sets in bedrooms, bathrooms, kitchens, cars, and now in pockets. Different programmes are provided for those engaged in diverse activities. Radio, once a form of group listening that emptied churches, has reverted to private and individual use since TV. The teenager withdraws from the TV group to his private radio.

This natural bias of radio to a close tie-in with diversified community groups is best manifested in the disk-jockey cults, and in radio's use of the telephone in a glorified form of the old trunkline wire-tapping. Plato, who had old-fashioned tribal ideas of political structure, said that the proper size of a city was indicated by the number of people who could hear the voice of a public speaker. Even the printed book, let alone radio, renders the political assumptions of Plato quite irrelevant for practical purposes. Yet radio, because of its ease of decentralized intimate relation with both private and small communities, could easily implement the Platonic political dream on a world scale.

The uniting of radio with phonograph that constitutes the average radio programme yields a very special pattern quite superior in power to the combination of radio and telegraph press that yields our news and weather programmes. It is curious how much more arresting are the weather reports than the news, on both radio and TV. Is not this because 'weather' is now entirely an electronic form of information, whereas news retains much of the pattern of the printed word? It is probably the print and book bias of the BBC and the CBC that renders them so awkward and inhibited in radio and TV presentation. Commercial urgency, rather than artistic insight, fostered by contrast a hectic vivacity in the corresponding American operation.

9 From: Understanding Media by Marshall McLuhan

Television

The Timid Giant

Perhaps the most familiar and pathetic effect of the TV image is the posture of children in the early grades. Since TV, children—regardless of eye condition—average about six and a half inches from the printed page. Our children are striving to carry over to the printed page the all-involving sensory mandate of the TV image. With perfect psycho-mimetic skill, they carry out the commands of the TV image. They pore, they probe, they slow down and involve themselves in depth. This is what they had learned to do in the cool iconography of the comic-book medium. TV carried the process much further. Suddenly they are transferred to the hot print medium with its uniform patterns and fast lineal movement. Pointlessly they strive to read print in depth. They bring to print all their senses, and print rejects them. Print asks for the isolated and stripped-down visual faculty, not for the unified sensorium.

The Mackworth head-camera, when worn by children watching TV, has revealed that their eyes follow, not the actions, but the reactions. The eyes scarcely deviate from the faces of the actors, even during scenes of violence. This head-camera shows by projection both the scene and the eye movement simultaneously. Such extraordinary behaviour is another indication of the very cool and involving character of this medium.

On the Jack Paar show for March 8, 1963, Richard Nixon was Paared down and remade into a suitable TV image. It turns out that Mr Nixon is both a pianist and a composer. With sure tact for the character of the TV medium, Jack Paar brought out this *pianoforte* side of Mr Nixon, with excellent effect. Instead of the slick, glib, legal Nixon, we saw the doggedly creative and modest performer. A few timely touches like this would have quite altered the result of the Kennedy–Nixon campaign. TV is a medium that rejects the sharp personality and favours the presentation of processes rather than of products.

The adaptation of TV to processes, rather than to the neatly packaged products, explains the frustration many people experience with this medium in its political uses. An article by Edith Efron in *TV Guide* (May 18–24, 1963) labelled TV 'The Timid Giant', because it is unsuited to hot issues and sharply defined controversial topics: 'Despite official freedom from censorship, a self-imposed silence renders network documentaries almost mute on many great issues of the day.' As a cool medium TV has, some feel, introduced a kind of *rigor mortis* into the body politic. It is the extraordinary degree of audience participation in the TV medium that explains its failure to tackle hot issues. Howard K. Smith observed: 'The networks are delighted if you go into a controversy in a country 14,000 miles away. They don't want real controversy, real dissent, at home.' For people conditioned to the hot newspaper medium, which is concerned with the clash of *views*, rather than involvement in *depth* in a situation, the TV behaviour is inexplicable.

Such a hot news item that concerns TV directly was headlined 'It finally happened—a British film with English subtitles to explain the dialects.' The film in question is the British comedy 'Sparrows Don't Sing'. A glossary of Yorkshire, Cockney, and other slang phrases has been printed for the customers so that they can figure out just what the subtitles mean. Sub subtitles are as handy an indicator of the depth effects of TV as the new 'rugged' styles in feminine attire. One of the most extraordinary developments since TV in England has been the upsurge of regional dialects. A regional brogue or 'burr' is the vocal equivalent of gaiter stockings. Such brogues undergo continual erosion from literacy. Their sudden prominence in England in areas in which previously one had heard only standard English is one of the most significant cultural events of our time. Even in the classrooms of Oxford and Cambridge, the local dialects are heard again. The undergraduates of those universities no longer strive to achieve a uniform speech. Dialectal speech since TV has been found to provide a social bond in depth, not possible with the artificial 'standard English' that began only a century ago.

An article on Perry Como bills him as 'Low-pressure king of a high-pressure realm'. The success of any TV performer depends on his achieving a low-pressure style of presentation, although getting his act on the air may require much high-pressure organization. Castro may be a case in point. According to Tad

Szulc's story on 'Cuban Television's One-man Show' (*The Eighth Art*), 'in his seemingly improvised "as-I-go-along" style he can evolve politics and govern his country—right on camera'. Now, Tad Szulc is under the illusion that TV is a hot medium, and suggests that in the Congo 'television might have helped Lumumba to incite the masses to even great turmoil and bloodshed'. But he is quite wrong. Radio is the medium for frenzy, and it has been the major means of hotting up the tribal blood of Africa, India and China, alike. TV has cooled Cuba down, as it is cooling down America. What the Cubans are getting by TV is the experience of being directly engaged in the making of political decisions. Castro presents himself as a teacher, and as Szulc says, 'manages to blend political guidance and education with propaganda so skillfully that it is often difficult to tell where one begins and the other ends'. Exactly the same mix is used in entertainment in Europe and America alike. Seen outside the United States, any American movie looks like subtle political propaganda. Acceptable entertainment has to flatter and exploit the cultural and political assumptions of the land of its origin. Those unspoken presuppositions also serve to blind people to the most obvious facts about a new medium like TV.

In a group of simulcasts of several media done in Toronto a few years back, TV did a strange flip. Four randomized groups of university students were given the same information at the same time about the structure of preliterate languages. One group received it via radio, one from TV, one by lecture, and one read it. For all but the reader group, the information was passed along in straight verbal flow by the same speaker without discussion or questions or use of blackboard. Each group had half an hour of exposure to the material. Each was asked to fill in the same quiz afterward. It was quite a surprise to the experimenters when the students performed better with TV-channelled information and with radio than they did with lecture and print—and the TV group stood *well* above the radio group. Since nothing had been done to give special stress to any of these four media, the experiment was repeated with other randomized groups. This time each medium was allowed full opportunity to do its stuff. For radio and TV, the material was dramatized with many auditory and visual features. The lecturer took full advantage of the blackboard and class discussion. The printed form was embellished with an imaginative use of typography and page layout to stress each point in the lecture. All of these media had been stepped up to high intensity for this repeat of the original performance. Television and radio once again showed results high above lecture and print. Unexpectedly to the testers, however, radio now stood significantly above television. It was a long time before the obvious reason declared itself, namely that TV is a cool, participant medium. When hotted up by dramatization and stingers, it performs less well because there is less opportunity for participation. Radio is a hot medium. When given additional intensity, it performs better. It doesn't invite the same degree of participation in its users. Radio will serve as background-sound or as noise-level control, as when the ingenious teenager employs it as a means of privacy. TV will not work as background. It engages you. You have to be *with* it. (The phrase has gained acceptance since TV.)

A great many things will not work since the arrival of TV. Not only the movies, but the national magazines as well, have been hit very hard by this new medium. Even the comic books have declined greatly. Before TV, there had been much concern about why Johnny couldn't read. Since TV, Johnny has acquired an entirely new set of perceptions. He is not at all the same. Otto Preminger, director of *Anatomy of a Murder* and other hits, dates a great change in movie making and viewing from the very first year of general TV programming. 'In 1951,' he wrote, 'I started a fight to get the release in motion-picture theaters of *The Moon Is Blue* after the production code approval was refused. It was a small fight and I won it.' (*Toronto Daily Star*, October 19, 1963.)

He went on to say, 'The very fact that it was the word "virgin" that was objected to in *The Moon Is Blue* is today laughable, almost incredible.' Otto Preminger considers that American movies have advanced toward maturity owing to the influence of TV. The cool TV medium promotes depth structures in art and entertainment alike, and creates audience involvement in depth as well. Since nearly all our technologies and entertainment since Gutenberg have been not cool, but hot; and not deep, but fragmentary; not producer-oriented, but consumer-oriented, there is scarcely a single area of established relationships, from home and church to school and market, that has not been profoundly disturbed in its pattern and texture.

The psychic and social disturbance created by the TV image, and not the TV programming, occasions daily comment in the press. Raymond Burr, who plays Perry Mason, spoke to the National Association of Municipal Judges, reminding them that, 'Without our laymen's understanding and acceptance, the laws which you apply and the courts in which you preside cannot continue to exist.' What Mr Burr omitted to observe was that the

67

Perry Mason TV programme, in which he plays the lead, is typical of that intensely participational kind of TV experience that has altered our relation to the laws and the courts.

The mode of the TV image has nothing in common with film or photo, except that it offers also a non-verbal *gestalt* or posture of forms. With TV, the viewer is the screen. He is bombarded with light impulses that James Joyce called the 'Charge of the Light Brigade' that imbues his 'soulskin with sobconscious inklings'. The TV image is visually low in data. The TV image is not a *still* shot. It is not photo in any sense, but a ceaselessly forming contour of things limned by the scanning-finger. The resulting plastic contour appears by light *through*, not light *on*, and the image so formed has the quality of sculpture and icon, rather than of picture. The TV image offers some three million dots per second to the receiver. From these he accepts only a few dozen each instant, from which to make an image.

The film image offers many more millions of data per second, and the viewer does not have to make the same drastic reduction of items to form his impression. He tends instead to accept the full image as a package deal. In contrast, the viewer of the TV mosaic, with technical control of the image, unconsciously reconfigures the dots into an abstract work of art on the pattern of a Seurat or Rouault. If anybody were to ask whether all this would change if technology stepped up the character of the TV image to movie data level, one could only counter by inquiring, 'Could we alter a cartoon by adding details of perspective and light and shade?' The answer is 'Yes', only it would then no longer be a cartoon. Nor would 'improved' TV be television. The TV image is *now* a mosaic mesh of light and dark spots which a movie shot never is, even when the quality of the movie image is very poor.

As in any other mosaic, the third dimension is alien to TV, but it can be superimposed. In TV the illusion of the third dimension is provided slightly by the stage sets in the studio; but the TV image itself is a flat two-dimensional mosaic. Most of the three-dimensional illusion is a carry-over of habitual viewing of film and photo. For the TV camera does not have a built-in angle of vision like the movie camera. Eastman Kodak now has a two-dimensional camera that can match the flat effects of the TV camera. Yet is is hard for literate people, with their habit of fixed points of view and three-dimensional vision, to understand the properties of two-dimensional vision. If it had been easy for them, they would have had no difficulties with abstract art, General Motors would not have made a mess of motor-car design, and the picture magazine would not be having difficulties now with the relationship between features and ads. The TV image requires each instant that we 'close' the spaces in the mesh by a convulsive sensuous participation that is profoundly kinetic and tactile, because tactility is the interplay of the senses, rather than the isolated contact of skin and object.

To contrast it with the film shot, many directors refer to the TV image as one of 'low definition', in the sense that it offers little detail and a low degree of information, much like the cartoon. A TV close-up provides only as much information as a small section of a long-shot on the movie screen. For lack of observing so central an aspect of the TV image, the critics of programme 'content' have talked nonsense about 'TV violence'. The spokesmen of censorious views are typically semiliterate book-oriented individuals who have no competence in the grammars of newspaper, or radio, or of film, but who look askew and askance at all non-book media. The simplest question about any psychic aspect, even of the book medium, throws these people into a panic of uncertainty. Vehemence of projection of a single isolated attitude they mistake for moral vigilance. Once these censors became aware that in all cases 'the medium is the message' or the basic source of effects, they would turn to suppression of media as such, instead of seeking 'content' control. Their current assumption that content or programming is the factor that influences outlook and action is derived from the book medium, with its sharp cleavage between form and content.

Is it not strange that TV should have been as revolutionary a medium in America in the 1950s as radio in Europe in the 1930s? Radio, the medium that resuscitated the tribal and kinship webs of the European mind in the 1920s and 1930s, had no such effect in England or America. There, the erosion of tribal bonds by means of literacy and its industrial extensions had gone so far that our radio did not achieve any notable tribal reactions. Yet ten years of TV have Europeanized even the United States, as witness its changed feelings for space and personal relations. There is new sensitivity to the dance, plastic arts, and architecture, as well as the demand for the small car, the paperback, sculptural hairdos and moulded dress effects—to say nothing of a new concern for complex effects in cuisine and in the use of wines. Notwithstanding, it would be misleading to say that TV will retribalize England and America. The action of radio on the world of resonant speech and memory was hysterical. But TV has certainly made England and America vulnerable to radio where previously they had immunity to a great degree. For good or ill, the TV image has exerted a unifying synesthetic force on the sense-life of these intensely literate populations, such as they have lacked for centuries. It is wise to withhold all value judgments when studying these media matters, since their effects are not capable of being isolated.

Synesthesia, or unified sense and imaginative life, had long seemed an unattainable dream to Western poets, painters, and artists in general. They had looked with sorrow and dismay on the fragmented and impoverished imaginative life of Western literate man in the eighteenth century and later. Such was the message of Blake and Pater, Yeats and D. H. Lawrence, and a host of other great figures. They were not prepared to have their dreams realized in everyday life by the esthetic action of radio and television. Yet these massive extensions of our central nervous systems have enveloped Western man in a daily session of synesthesia. The Western way of life attained centuries since by the rigorous separation and specialization of the senses, with the visual sense atop the hierarchy, is not able to withstand the radio and TV waves that wash about the great visual structure of abstract Individual Man. Those who, from political motives, would now add their force to the anti-individual action of our electric technology are puny subliminal automatons aping the patterns of the prevailing electric pressures. A century ago they would, with equal somnambulism, have faced in the opposite direction. German Romantic poets and philosophers had been chanting in tribal chorus for a return to the dark unconscious for over a century before radio and Hitler made such a return difficult to avoid. What is to be thought of people who wish such a return to preliterate ways, when they have no inkling of how the civilized visual way was ever substituted for tribal auditory magic?

At this hour, when Americans are discovering new passions for skin-diving and the wraparound space of small cars, thanks to the indomitable tactile promptings of the TV image, the same image is inspiring many English people with race feelings of tribal exclusiveness. Whereas highly literate Westerners have always idealized the condition of integration of races, it has been their literate culture that made impossible real uniformity among races. Literate man naturally dreams of visual solutions to the problems of human differences. At the end of the nineteenth century, this kind of dream suggested similar dress and education for both men and women. The failure of the sex-integration programmes has provided the theme of much of the literature and psychoanalysis of the twentieth century. Race integration, undertaken on the basis of visual uniformity, is an extension of the same cultural strategy of literate man, for whom differences always seem to need eradication, both in sex and in race, and in space and in time. Electronic man, by becoming ever more deeply involved in the actualities of the human condition, cannot accept the literate cultural strategy. The Negro will reject a plan of visual uniformity as definitely as women did earlier, and for the same reasons. Women found that they had been robbed of their distinctive roles and turned into fragmented citizens in 'a man's world'. The entire approach to these problems in terms of uniformity and social homogenization is a final pressure of the mechanical and industrial technology. Without moralizing, it can be said that the electric age, by involving all men deeply in one another, will come to reject such mechanical solutions. It is more difficult to provide uniqueness and diversity than it is to impose the uniform patterns of mass education; but it is such uniqueness and diversity that can be fostered under electric conditions as never before.

Temporarily, all preliterature groups in the world have begun to feel the explosive and aggressive energies that are released by the onset of the new literacy and mechanization. These explosions come just at a time when the new electric technology combines to make us share them on a global scale.

The effect of TV, as the most recent and spectacular electric extension of our central nervous system, is hard to grasp for various reasons. Since it has affected the totality of our lives, personal and social and political, it would be quite unrealistic to attempt a 'systematic' or visual presentation of such influence. Instead, it is more feasible to 'present' TV as a complex *gestalt* of data gathered almost at random.

The TV image is of low intensity or definition, and, therefore, unlike film, it does not afford detailed information about objects. The difference is akin to that between the old manuscripts and the printed word. Print gave intensity and uniform prevision, where before there had been a diffuse texture. Print brought in the taste for exact measurement and repeatability that we now associate with science and mathematics.

The TV producer will point out that speech on television must not have the careful precision necessary in the theatre. The TV actor does not have to project either his voice or himself. Likewise, TV acting is so extremely intimate, because of the peculiar involvement of the viewer with the completion or 'closing' of the TV image, that the actor must achieve a great degree of spontaneous casualness that would be irrelevant in movie and lost on stage. For the audience participates in the inner life of the TV actor as fully as in the outer life of the movie star. Technically, TV tends to be a close-up medium. The close-up that in the movie is used for shock is, on TV, a quite casual thing. And whereas a glossy photo the size of the TV screen would show a dozen faces in adequate detail, a dozen faces on the TV screen are only a blur.

The peculiar character of the TV image in its relation to the actor causes such familiar reactions as our not being able to recognize in real life a person whom we see every week on TV. Not many of us are as alert as the kindergartener who said to Garry Moore, 'How did you get off TV?' Newscasters and actors alike report the frequency with which they are approached by people who feel they've met them before. Joanne Woodward in an interview was asked what was the difference between being a movie star and a TV actress. She replied: 'When I was in the movies I heard people say, "There goes Joanne Woodward". Now they say, "There goes somebody I think I know".'

The owner of a Hollywood hotel in an area where many movie and TV actors reside reported that tourists had switched their allegiance to TV stars. Moreover, most TV stars are men, that is, 'cool characters', while most movie stars are women, since they can be presented as 'hot' characters. Men and women movie stars alike, along with the entire star system, have tended to dwindle into a more moderate status since TV. The movie is a hot, high-definition medium. Perhaps the most interesting observation of the hotel proprietor was that the tourists wanted to see Perry Mason and Wyatt Earp. They did not want to see Raymond Burr and Hugh O'Brian. The old movie-fan tourists had wanted to see their favourites as they were in *real* life, not as they were in their film roles. The fans of the cool TV medium want to see their star in *role*, whereas the movie fans want the *real thing*.

A similar reversal of attitudes occurred with the printed book. There was little interest in the private lives of authors under manuscript or scribal culture. Today the comic strip is close to the pre-print woodcut and manuscript form of expression. Walt Kelly's *Pogo* looks very much indeed like a gothic page. Yet in spite of great public interest in the comic-strip form, there is as little curiosity about the private lives of these artists as about the lives of popular-song writers. With print, the private life became of the utmost concern to readers. Print is a hot medium. It projects the author at the public as the movie did. The manuscript is a cool medium that does not project the author, so much as involve the reader. So with TV. The viewer is involved and participant. The *role* of the TV star, in this way, seems more fascinating than his private life. It is thus that the student of media, like the psychiatrist, gets more data from his informants than they themselves have perceived. Everybody experiences far more than he understands. Yet it is experience, rather than understanding, that influences behaviour, especially in collective matters of media and technology, where the individual is almost inevitably unaware of their effect upon him.

Some may find it paradoxical that a cool medium like TV should be so much more compressed and condensed than a hot medium like film. But it is well known that a half minute of television is equal to three minutes of stage or vaudeville. The same is true of manuscript in contrast to print. The 'cool' manuscript tended toward compressed forms of statement, aphoristic and allegorical. The 'hot' print medium expanded expression in the direction of simplification and the 'spelling-out' of meanings. Print speeded up and 'exploded' the compressed script into simpler fragments.

A cool medium, whether the spoken word or the manuscript or TV, leaves much more for the listener or user to do than a hot medium. If the medium is of high definition, participation is low. If the medium is of low intensity, the participation is high. Perhaps this is why lovers mumble so.

Because the low definition of TV insures a high degree of audience involvement, the most effective programmes are those that present situations which consist of some process to be completed. Thus, to use TV to teach poetry would permit the teacher to concentrate on the poetic process of actual *making*, as it pertained to a particular poem. The book form is quite unsuited to this type of involved presentation. The same salience of process of do-it-yourself-ness and depth involvement in the TV image extends to the art of the TV actor. Under TV conditions, he must be alert to improvise and to embellish every phrase and verbal resonance with details of gesture and posture, sustaining that intimacy with the viewer which is not possible on the massive movie screen or on the stage.

There is the alleged remark of the Nigerian who, after seeing a TV western, said delightedly, 'I did not realize you valued human life so little in the West.' Offsetting this remark is the behaviour of our children in watching TV westerns. When equipped with the new experimental head-cameras that follow their eye movements while watching the image, children keep their eyes on the faces of the TV actors. Even during physical violence their eyes remain concentrated on the facial *reactions*, rather than on the eruptive *action*. Guns, knives, fists, all are ignored in preference for the facial expression. TV is not so much an action, as a re-action, medium.

The yen of the TV medium for themes of process and complex reactions has enabled the documentary type of film to come to the fore. The movie *can* handle process superbly, but the movie viewer is more disposed to be a passive consumer of actions, rather than a participant of reactions. The movie western, like the movie documentary, has always been a lowly form. With TV the western acquired new importance, since its theme is always: 'Let's make a town.' The audience participates in the shaping and processing of a community from meagre and unpromising components. Moreover, the TV image takes kindly to the varied and rough textures of Western saddles, clothes, hides, and shoddy match-wood bars and hotel lobbies. The movie camera, by contrast, is at home in the slick chrome world of the night club and the luxury spots of a metropolis. Moreover, the contrasting camera preferences of the movies in the Twenties and Thirties, and of TV in the Fifties and Sixties spread to the entire population. In ten years the new tastes of America in clothes, in food, in housing, in entertainment, and in vehicles express the new pattern of interrelation of forms and do-it-yourself involvement fostered by the TV image.

It is no accident that such major movie stars as Rita Hayworth, Liz Taylor, and Marilyn Monroe ran into troubled waters in the new TV age. They ran into an age that questioned all the 'hot' media values of the pre-TV consumer days. The TV image challenges the values of fame as much as the values of consumer goods. 'Fame to me,' said Marilyn Monroe, 'certainly is only a temporary and a partial happiness. Fame is not really for a daily diet, that's not what fulfills you. . . . I think that when you are famous every weakness is exaggerated. This industry should behave to its stars like a mother whose child has just run out in front of a car. But instead of clasping the child to them they start punishing the child.'

The movie community is now getting clobbered by TV, and lashes out at anybody in its bewildered petulance. These words of the great movie puppet who wed Mr Baseball and Mr Broadway are surely a portent. If many of the rich and successful figures in America were to question publicly the absolute value of money and success as means to happiness and human welfare, they would offer no more shattering a precedent than Marilyn Monroe. For nearly fifty years, Hollywood had offered 'the fallen woman' a way to the top and a way to the hearts of all. Suddenly the love-goddess emits a horrible cry, screams that eating people is wrong, and utters denunciations of the whole way of life. This is exactly the mood of the suburban beatniks. They reject a fragmented and specialist consumer life for anything that offers humble involvement and deep commitment. It is the same mood that recently turned girls from specialist careers to early marriage and big families. They switch from jobs to roles.

The same new preference for depth participation has also prompted in the young a strong drive toward religious experience with rich liturgical overtones. The liturgical revival of the radio and TV age affects even the most austere Protestant sects. Choral chant and rich vestments have appeared in every quarter. The ecumenical movement is synonymous with electric technology.

Just as TV, the mosaic mesh, does not foster perspective in art, it does not foster lineality in living. Since TV, the assembly line has disappeared from industry. Staff and line structures have dissolved in management. Gone are the stag line, the party line, the receiving line, and the pencil line from the backs of nylons.

With TV came the end of bloc voting in politics, a form of specialism and fragmentation that won't work since TV. Instead of the voting bloc, we have the icon, the inclusive image. Instead of a political viewpoint or platform, the inclusive political posture or stance. Instead of the product, the process. In periods of new and rapid growth there is a blurring of outlines. In the TV image we have the supremacy of the blurred outline, itself the maximal incentive to growth and new 'closure' or completion, especially for a consumer culture long related to the sharp visual values that had become separated from the other senses. So great is the change in American lives, resulting from the loss of loyalty to the consumer package in entertainment and commerce, that every enterprise, from Madison Avenue and General Motors to Hollywood and General Foods, has been shaken thoroughly and forced to seek new strategies of action. What electric implosion or contraction has done inter-personally and inter-nationally, the TV image does intra-personally or intra-sensuously.

It is not hard to explain this sensuous revolution to painters and sculptors, for they have been striving, ever since Cézanne abandoned perspective illusion in favour of structure in painting, to bring about the very change that TV has now effected on a fantastic scale. TV is the Bauhaus programme of design and living, or the Montessori educational strategy, given total technological extension and commercial sponsorship. The aggressive lunge of artistic strategy for the remaking of Western man has, *via* TV, become a vulgar sprawl and an overwhelming splurge in American life. . . .

WHY THE TV CHILD CANNOT SEE AHEAD

The plunge into depth experience via the TV image can only be explained in terms of the differences between visual and mosaic space. Ability to discriminate between these radically different forms is quite rare in our Western world. It has been pointed out that, in the country of the blind, the one-eyed man is not king. He is taken to be an hallucinated lunatic. In a highly visual culture, it is as difficult to communicate the nonvisual properties of spatial forms as to explain visuality to the blind. In the ABC of Relativity Bertrand Russell began by explaining that there is nothing difficult about Einstein's ideas, but that they do call for total reorganization of our imaginative lives. It is precisely this imaginative reorganization that has occurred via the TV image.

The ordinary inability to discriminate between the photographic and the TV image is not merely a crippling factor in the learning process today; it is symptomatic of an age-old failure in Western culture. The literate man, accustomed to an environment in which the visual sense is extended everywhere as a principle of organization, sometimes supposes that the mosaic world of primitive art, or even the world of Byzantine art, represents a mere difference in degree, a sort of failure to bring their visual portrayals up to the level of full visual effectiveness. Nothing could be further from the truth. This, in fact, is a misconception that has impaired understanding between East and West for many centuries. Today it impairs relations between coloured and white societies.

Most technology produces an amplification that is quite explicit in its separation of the senses. Radio is an extension of the aural, high-fidelity photography of the visual. But TV is, above all, an extension of the sense of touch, which involves maximal interplay of all the senses. For Western man, however, the all-embracing extension had occurred by means of phonetic writing, which is a technology for extending the sense of sight. All non-phonetic forms of writing are, by contrast, artistic modes that retain much variety of sensuous orchestration. Phonetic writing, alone, has the power of separating and fragmenting the senses and of sloughing off the semantic complexities. The TV image reverses this literate process of analytic fragmentation of sensory life.

The visual stress on continuity, uniformity, and connectedness, as it derives from literacy, confronts us with the great technological means of implementing continuity and lineality by fragmented repetition. The ancient world found this means in the brick, whether for wall or road. The repetitive, uniform brick, indispensable agent of road and wall, of cities and empires, is an extension, via letters, of the visual sense. *The brick wall is not a mosaic form*, and neither is the mosaic form a visual structure. The mosaic can be *seen* as dancing can, but is not *structured* visually; nor is it an extension of the visual power. For the mosaic is not uniform, continuous, or repetitive. It is discontinuous, skew, and nonlineal, like the tactual TV image. To the sense of touch, all things are sudden, counter, original, spare, strange. The 'Pied Beauty' of G. M. Hopkins is a catalogue of the notes of the sense of touch. The poem is a manifesto of the nonvisual, and like Cézanne or Seurat, or Rouault it provides an indispensable approach to understanding TV. The nonvisual mosaic structures of modern art, like those of modern physics and electric-information patterns, permit little detachment. The mosaic form of the TV image demands participation and involvement in depth of the whole being, as does the sense of touch. Literacy, in contrast, had, by extending the visual power to the uniform organization of time and space, psychically and socially, conferred the power of detachment and noninvolvement.

The visual sense when extended by phonetic literacy fosters the analytic habit of perceiving the single facet in the life of forms. The visual power enables us to isolate the single incident in time and space, as in representational art. In visual representation of a person or an object, a single phase or moment or aspect is separated from the multitude of known and felt phases, moments and aspects of the person or object. By contrast, iconographic art uses the eye as we use our hand in seeking to create an inclusive image, made up of many moments, phases, and aspects of the person or thing. Thus the iconic mode is not visual representation, nor the specialization of visual stress as defined by viewing from a single position. The tactual mode of perceiving is sudden but not specialist. It is total, synesthetic, involving all the senses. Pervaded by the mosaic TV image, the TV child encounters the world in a spirit antithetic to literacy.

The TV image, that is to say, even more than the icon, is an extension of the sense of touch. Where it encounters a literate culture, it necessarily thickens the sense-mix, transforming fragmented and specialist extensions into a seamless web of experience. Such transformation is, of course, a 'disaster' for a literate, specialist culture. It blurs many cherished attitudes and procedures. It dims the efficacy of the basic pedagogic techniques, and the relevance of the curriculum. If for no other reason, it would be well to understand the dynamic life of these forms as they intrude upon us and upon one another. TV makes for myopia.

The young people who have experienced a decade of TV have naturally imbibed an urge toward involvement in depth that makes all the remote visualized goals of usual culture seem not only unreal but irrelevant, and not only irrelevant but anaemic. It is the total involvement in all-inclusive *nowness* that occurs in young lives via TV's mosaic image. This change of attitude has nothing to do with programming in any way, and would be the same if the programmes consisted entirely of the highest cultural content. The change in attitude by means of relating themselves to the mosaic TV image would occur in any event. It is, of course, our job not only to understand this change but to exploit it for its pedagogical richness. The TV child expects involvement and doesn't want a specialist *job* in the future. He does want a *role* and a deep commitment to his society. Unbridled and misunderstood, this richly human need can manifest itself in the distorted forms portrayed in *West Side Story*.

The TV child cannot see ahead because he wants involvement, and he cannot accept a fragmentary and merely visualized goal or destiny in learning or in life.

MURDER BY TELEVISION

Jack Ruby shot Lee Oswald while tightly surrounded by guards who were paralysed by television cameras. The fascinating and involving power of television scarcely needed this additional proof of its peculiar operation upon human perceptions. The Kennedy assassination gave people an immediate sense of the television power to create depth involvement, on the one hand, and a numbing effect as deep as grief, itself, on the other hand. Most people were amazed at the depth of meaning which the event communicated to them. Many more were surprised by the coolness and calm of the mass reaction. The same event, handled by press or radio (in the absence of television), would have provided a totally different experience. The national 'lid' would have 'blown off'. Excitement would have been enormously greater and depth participation in a common awareness very much less.

As explained earlier, Kennedy was an excellent TV image. He had used the medium with the same effectiveness that Roosevelt had learned to achieve by radio. With TV, Kennedy found it natural to involve the nation in the office of the Presidency both as an operation and as an image. TV reaches out for the corporate attributes of office. Potentially, it can transform the Presidency into a monarchic dynasty. A merely elective Presidency scarcely affords the depth of dedication and commitment demanded by the TV form. Even teachers on TV seem to be endowed by the student audiences with a charismatic or mystic character that much exceeds the feelings developed in the classroom or lecture hall. In the course of many studies of audience reactions to TV teaching, there recurs this puzzling fact. The viewers feel that the teacher has a dimension almost of sacredness. This feeling does not have its basis in concepts or ideas, but seems to creep in uninvited and unexplained. It baffles both the students and the analysts of their reactions. Surely, there could be no more telling touch to tip us off to the character of TV. This is not so much a visual as a tactual-auditory medium that involves all of our senses in depth interplay. For people long accustomed to the merely visual experience of the typographic and photographic varieties, it would seem to be the *synesthesia*, or tactual depth of TV experience, that dislocates them from their usual attitudes of passivity and detachment.

The banal and ritual remark of the conventionally literate, that TV presents an experience for passive viewers, is wide of the mark. TV is above all a medium that demands a creatively participant response. The guards who failed to protect Lee Oswald were not passive. They were so involved by the mere sight of the TV camera that they lost their sense of their merely practical and specialist task.

Perhaps it was the Kennedy funeral that most strongly impressed the audience with the power of TV to invest an occasion with the character of corporate participation. No national event except in sports has ever had such coverage or such an audience. It revealed the unrivalled power of TV to achieve the involvement of the audience in a complex *process*. The funeral as a corporate process caused even the image of sport to pale and dwindle into puny proportions. The Kennedy funeral, in short, manifested the power of TV to involve an entire population in a ritual process.

79

By comparison, press, movie and even radio are mere packaging devices for consumers.

Most of all, the Kennedy event provides an opportunity for noting a paradoxical feature of the 'cool' TV medium. It involves us in moving depth, but it does not excite, agitate or arouse. Presumably, this is a feature of all depth experience.

10 From: Report of the Committee on Broadcasting 1960

(i) *The purposes of broadcasting*

41. As we have already noted, the disquiet about television derived from the view that the power of the medium to influence and persuade is immense. This assessment is widely regarded as being self-evident; but, since it lies at the root of much that is said and thought about the conduct of the television services, we examined it closely. Some found a striking expression of their views in the assertion of the Beveridge Committee ten years before that 'broadcasting is the most pervasive, and therefore one of the most powerful of agents for influencing men's thoughts and actions'. Many drew attention to the special characteristics of television: to its capacity for dramatic presentation and so for exemplifying in a specially effective way the thoughts and actions of living people, to the transience of its pictorial statements, and to the consequent difficulty of analysing and criticizing them. If the medium has unique characteristics, so too have television audiences. Many submissions drew attention to the vast size of the audiences for many programme items; audiences of over eighteen millions are not unusual and of twelve millions relatively common. Another characteristic often attributed to television audiences was, in the words of the Workers' Educational Association, their vulnerability. 'Going to a cinema or a theatre, buying or borrowing a book or a magazine involve a conscious critical approach', said the Association; by contrast, 'The television audience is vulnerable to influence in a way that readers of

newspapers and cinema audiences are not.' Sitting at home, people are relaxed, less consciously critical and, therefore, more exposed. Further, audiences are often family groups and include children who are normally protected from outside influences, and therefore especially vulnerable. Many submissions emphasized how the power of television was due largely to the unique way in which it brought actuality, or the appearance of actuality, into the home. This point was most effectively made by a spokesman of the Proprietary Association of Great Britain, who said this to us: 'The best way to sell the goods is to put a man in the home. The nearest you can get to that is television.'

42. We cannot say that this assessment of the power of the medium is proved. So far, there is little conclusive evidence on the effects of television on values and moral attitudes. But those who work professionally in this sphere told us that what evidence there was, showed that there was an effect. We were told that this effect, good or bad, need not be sudden or spectacular. Rather it was to be compared with that of water dripping on a stone: persistent, apparently imperceptible, but in the end prevailing. It may be that in this sphere cause and effect can never be absolutely demonstrable. But there must be a presumption one way or the other on which to found policies for the conduct of the services, and against which to measure the responsibilities of those who provide them. The strong tide of opinion, explicit or implicit, in the submissions to us, leaves no doubt whatsoever what, in their authors' views, the presumption should be. Our own judgment, after weighing such evidence as is available to us, leads us to a clear conclusion. It is that, unless and until there is unmistakable proof to the contrary, the presumption must be that television is and will be a main factor in influencing the values and moral standards of our society. We strongly refute the argument that because an effect has not been conclusively proved the broadcasting authorities need not concern themselves with it. The measure of their responsibility is this: that by its nature, broadcasting must be in a constant and sensitive relationship with the moral condition of society. Broadcasters are, and must be, involved; this gives them a responsibility they cannot evade.

(ii) *Disquiet about TV*

81. As we have already noted, disquiet derived from an assessment, which we fully accept, that the power of the medium to influence and persuade is immense; and from a strong feeling, amounting often to a conviction, that very often the use of the

power suggested a lack of awareness of, or concern about, the consequences. The consideration which gave rise to this feeling was usually that, for the sake of easy appeal, television portrayed too often a world in which the moral standards normally accepted in society were either ignored or flouted, and that for a similar reason it showed excessive violence. There is no doubt that concern is widespread and acute. It cannot be dismissed as the unrepresentative opinion of a few well-meaning but over-anxious critics, still less as that of cranks. It has been represented to us from all parts of the kingdom and by many organizations of widely differing kinds: by political parties, women's clubs and associations, local authorities, religious denominations, educational bodies and others. The Association of Municipal Corporations, for example, told us that it concurred with the criticism commonly made of some television programmes—that they have been damaging in certain moral aspects, that too many have featured sordid, unsavoury and violent themes, and that they present a false picture of life as though it were normal. A report: 'Broadcasting: the next steps', published by the Conservative Political Centre was sent to us. For convenience we refer to its authors as 'an Independent Group of Conservatives'. The report detected growing signs which, it thought, producers would do well to heed, of public feeling on the subject of unsuitable programmes. The National Federation of Women's Institutes canvassed opinion thoughout its County Federations and was thus able to provide us with a firm assessment of the general opinion of members of the Institutes. A very large majority of the answers to its canvass protested about the amount of violence and crime portrayed in television. We quote these views here as representative of those advanced in the great majority of the submissions put to us. We could have quoted from many others. Further, the concern these views reflect was reinforced by the opinion of those experts in sociology and psychology who gave evidence to us on the probable effect of television on society. The experts agreed that the information available to them was very far from complete; but this was not to say that there was no information. Dr Hilde Himmelweit told us that all the evidence so far provided by detailed researches suggested that values were acquired, that a view of life was picked up, by children watching television. Professor Eysenck told us there were good theoretical grounds for supposing that moral standards could be affected by television, and that these grounds were largely supported by experimental and clinical evidence.

84. We deal first with violence. This was widely defined by those who criticized its portrayal as including not only physical violence, but also an unfeeling or cruel disposition of mind which might express itself in speech or apparently casual habits alone, and not necessarily in acts of overt violence. On the whole, the critics recognized that the stylized conventions to be found in Sherwood Forest or in Ruritania, or in the old-fashioned 'Cowboys and Indians' programme, robbed violence of much of its effect, and thought that such programmes were in themselves harmless. But this could not be said of some of the newer 'sophisticated' Westerns which depict recognizable psychological problems in an atmosphere of violence and brutality. And the constant repetition of even the most stylized scenes of violence was thought to be harmful.

85. Disquiet at the portrayal of violence was expressed on three main grounds. The first was that scenes of violence frightened small children, that small children were disturbed by any programmes which suggested a threat to the world which they knew and in which they felt secure; and that the most cruel threat was violence. The second was that such programmes might lead children to dangerous, and even disastrous, experiment. The third was that showing violence encouraged anti-social, callous and even vicious attitudes and behaviour. These three grounds were not always differentiated, for the same programme will affect different people differently. To show that it does not affect one part of the audience is not to show that it affects no other part. The disquiet was, then, about the general effect of violence, and it led to two main criticisms of programmes in which it featured. The first criticism was simply that too much violence was shown on television. Some put this criticism to us merely as an example of lack of balance—where time was limited, it was given undue prominence. But most claimed that it was the constant repetition of violence, rather than the fact that it was shown at all, which was damaging. The second main criticism was of the treatment of violence. Many submissions recorded the view that it was often used gratuitously, that it often did little or nothing to develop plot or characterization and that it was, presumably, thrown in 'for kicks'. Another common opinion was that it was often unnecessarily emphasized by being shown in close-up and by being lingered over. The damage was not necessarily repaired by ensuring that, in the end, the good were seen to win and the bad to lose, and that crime did not pay: conventional endings of this sort did not penetrate to the level at which the portrayal of

violence had its emotional effect. What mattered was that violence provided the emotional energy, the dramatic content, of the programme.

89. We have already noted that concern about the portrayal on television programmes of low standards of morals and behaviour is also general. Some submissions represented that alcohol was too often shown in television plays and serials as though it were a necessity of normal life. Still more common was the view that promiscuity and adultery were often shown as though they were normal behaviour and, more generally, that sex was exploited. These particular criticisms of violence and of low standards of morals and behaviour should not be considered in isolation. For some criticized television for showing too much drinking, sex and violence, while others told us that the fact that they so much appeared in programmes was symptomatic of a deeper-seated ill, of a comprehensive carelessness about moral standards generally. Some argued that this was an age in which traditional standards were increasingly in question and one in which, therefore, what everybody did set the standard; and that there was nothing which could so powerfully convey what everybody did as television. The difficulties which television faced were, therefore, real. It had a duty to mirror actual ways of life and habits, and to portray the honest doubts of independently minded people about traditional standards. But at the same time whatever it showed would help to create the prevailing moral climate and could therefore aggravate existing moral uncertainties and disorders. Broadcasters, we were told, should not, therefore, assume that attitude of scientific indifference to results which admits only two questions—what happens, and why. They must accept as part of their responsibility a constant and living relationship with the moral condition of society. Emphatically, this was not to say that where there was virtue, there could be no cakes and ale; that gloom was good and gaiety godless; that there could be no pleasure on Sundays. Nor was it to say that the sordid and harsh truth must not be shown. For television's picture of the world must be realistic, and people can come to suffer as much harm from being led to believe that there is no evil in the world, as from seeing it over-emphasized. Rather it was to say that, over the whole range of programming, treatment must not exploit moral weakness and uncertainties, and timing must recognize that in television's audience there are not only those whose standards are already set, but those whose standards are being shaped by what they see.

90. From the representations which have been put to us, this is

the underlying cause of the disquiet about television: the belief, deeply felt, that the way television has portrayed human behaviour and treated moral issues has already done something and will in time do much to worsen the moral climate of the country. That this is a time when many of the standards by which people have hitherto lived are often questioned is not in itself regrettable. But it is necessary that the questions should be fairly put and fairly answered. If, in much of television, our society is presented as having extensively answered those questions by rejecting the standards by which it has hitherto lived and by putting bad standards or none in their place, if our society is presented as having accepted that the appeals should be made to our worse rather than to our better selves, then the questions will not have been fairly put but will have been hopelessly prejudiced—for ill.

Triviality

97. On the general quality of television programmes, viewers expressed both disquiet and dissatisfaction. Indeed, one of the main impressions left with us by written submissions and spoken opinion is that much that is seen on television is regarded as of very little value. There was, we were told, a preoccupation in many programmes with the superficial, the cheaply sensational. Many mass appeal programmes were vapid and puerile, their content often derivative, repetitious and lacking in real substance. There was a vast amount of unworthy material, and to transmit it was to misuse intricate machinery and equipment, skill, ingenuity, and time. Their presentation, too, showed a lack of willingness to experiment. In all, one had to infer either that those who provided these programmes mistakenly assumed that popular taste was uniformly and irremediably low, and popular culture irresponsible; or worse, that they did not care about them.

98. All such criticisms were often summed up in the charge of 'triviality'. We should make clear what we understand is meant by 'triviality' in this context. Triviality is not necessarily related to the subject matter of a programme; it can appear in drama, current affairs programmes, religious programmes or sports programmes just as easily as in light comedy or variety shows. One programme may be gay and frivolous—as light as a soufflé— and yet not be trivial. Another programme may seek prestige because it deals with intellectual or artistic affairs—and yet be trivial in its grasp or treatment; it may, for example, rely for its

appeal on technical tricks or the status of its compere, rather than on the worth of the subject matter, and the depth of its treatment. Triviality resides in the way the subject matter is approached and the manner in which it is presented.

99. A trivial approach can consist in a failure to respect the potentialities of the subject matter, no matter what it be, or in a too ready reliance on well-tried themes, or in a habit of conforming to established patterns, or in a reluctance to be imaginatively adventurous. A trivial presentation may consist in a failure to take full and disciplined advantage of the artistic and technical facilities which are relevant to a particular subject, or in an excessive interest in smart 'packaging' at the expense of the contents of the package, or in a reliance on 'gimmicks' so as to give a spurious interest to a programme at the cost of its imaginative integrity, or in too great a dependence on hackneyed devices for creating suspense or raising a laugh or evoking tears.

100. In short, there is no such thing as a trivial programme in the abstract. One should add, though, that television has created some forms of programme which particularly lend themselves to triviality, which lend themselves to the exploitation of artificial situations or of 'personalities' but have practically no subject matter or body of their own. Some quiz-shows and panel games obviously come into this category. But most trivial programmes —and we repeat that they may occur at any point across the range of different programmes—are programmes which have been trivialized by a defective approach, or a defective presentation, or both.

(iii) *A general appraisal of the television service of the BBC*

114. That the BBC is acutely aware of the power of the medium and regards itself as answerable for the general influence it exerts is, in our view, clear. Giving oral evidence, Mr Carleton Greene, Director General of the BBC, considered that television would be one of the main factors influencing the values and moral attitudes of our society. We need only add that nothing in the Corporation's written and oral evidence has suggested that they hold any reservations about the principle.

115. On the range and content of programmes, the BBC told us that the service should be comprehensive, and that a proper definition of 'comprehensive' must give enough weight to education and information. The Corporation regularly and deliberately put on programmes which would appeal immediately to a

comparatively small audience, but tried so to present them as to attract and hold wider audiences which did not at first know that they would be attracted by such programmes. 'But,' Mr Carleton Greene added, 'we should try always to do the best we possibly can in every type of broadcast, without thinking that it is more important to put our best into information and education. It is just as important to put the best skills one can into entertainment.' The BBC held it an important part of their responsibility to 'give a lead' to public taste, in literature and the arts and elsewhere. There was in this a risk of paternalism, but it was a risk of which they were conscious and which they must accept. The three elements—information, education and entertainment—were not separable: programmes which, if they must be classified would fall under the first two headings, were often, nevertheless, entertaining. Because the success of their service was not to be measured merely by the size of audiences, the BBC were themselves constantly questioning and testing their own programme policies. Also they engaged in continuous audience research to find out not only how many people watched programmes, but how they valued them. The response of the audience to a programme, the strength of its appreciation, was as important, if not more important, than the size of the audience. And further, for all their research, they would not claim they knew 'what the public wanted'; they reminded us that there must be experiment, trial and error.

123. On drama, the BBC told us that, just as it would be misleading to portray modern society as though it were never violent, so also would it be misleading to show it without its moral faults. But again, the faults should not be emphasized by showing them too often: still less should the treatment of particular programmes sensationalize them. Thus, the BBC told us that they had made a mistake in putting on a number of plays by young dramatists on successive Sunday nights. These had been 'kitchen-sink' plays: overall the emphasis had rested heavily on the sordid and sleazy. The mistake, Mr Adam (Director of Television Broadcasting) stated, lay in showing the plays in rapid succession. It had been one of programme planning, accentuated by the fact that comedies commissioned as part of the series had fallen by the way. There was, however, another and more important side to the coin, as we heard both from the BBC and from independent television. The BBC put it to us that, as a major patron of the drama, they had a positive responsibility to produce work of dramatic quality; if the creative impulse of the best young playwrights of today was

towards a particular kind of domestic tragedy, then the BBC had a duty to give it an outlet. If this meant that too high a proportion of new plays consisted of domestic tragedy, then the BBC would not, to provide variety, try to persuade dramatists to write less of these plays, and to turn to comedy, but would if necessary fill in with comedies from other periods. We record here our opinion that the BBC's sense of its responsibility is right, and its policies well conceived. On the one hand, the BBC should not attempt to muzzle or direct dramatists; and if, for example, 'kitchen-sink' drama seems to be a significant development in British dramatic writing, the BBC must be ready to show it. On the other, there is a responsibility to cater for the very varied tastes of the viewing public, and this must influence the time and occasion for showing plays of this kind.

127. The BBC told us that their traditional policy had been 'to develop programmes over the widest possible range of content and treatment, while preserving a reasonable balance between programmes intended for relaxation and amusement and those of a more thoughtful kind'. It was on range of subject matter presented and variety of treatment of particular subjects within that range that the primary emphasis lay. It was by extending the range of subject matter treated and the variety of treatment that the broadcaster developed the possibilities of the medium and increased its value. Also important was the ratio of relaxing —or 'light'—programmes to more demanding—or 'serious'— programmes: but this was not easily measured because 'light' and 'serious' were subjective terms. Nevertheless, most programmes were in practice recognizable as light or serious. The following kinds of programme might be classed as serious: news and current affairs, talks and discussions, documentary programmes, outside broadcasts of national importance and other major events of a non-sporting character, music (other than 'light music'), opera, ballet and religious programmes. Though some plays would be classed as serious programmes, others would not; so all were omitted from the class.

128. The BBC also told us that it was the core of their programme policy that the more important serious programmes should, for the most part, be offered when the largest audiences were available. This was between 7 p.m. and 10.30 p.m.—in peak viewing hours. The following table, compiled by the BBC, shows the percentage of peak viewing time over three recent years given to serious programmes (defined as in the preceding paragraph) in the BBC's programme.

Percentage of Peak Viewing Hours given to Serious Programmes
(excluding Drama) in the BBC Television Programme

January–June, 1958	.. ..	35
July–December, 1958	..	33
January–June, 1959	.. ..	$33\frac{1}{2}$
July–December, 1959	..	33
January–June, 1960	.. ..	$33\frac{1}{2}$
July–December, 1960	..	31

129. Mr Carleton Greene said that the Corporation's policy was to devote about one-third of peak viewing hours to serious programmes. If drama were included—and it was notoriously difficult to classify—the proportion was about one-half. He rejected the suggestion that the BBC would have exercised its responsibility in a more democratic way by giving much more of the peak viewing hours period to programmes which, intended for relaxation, would attract large audiences. Peak viewing hours were the time when most people were at home and had the opportunity of watching television. The effect of increasing the amount of peak viewing time given to light programmes would be to deprive very large audiences, even if they were not yet 'majority' audiences, of programmes they positively liked.

132. We are left in no doubt that the BBC's concept of balance and quality is sound—both in the range and treatment of subject matter, and in timing. From the representations put to us, we are satisfied that within the limits of a single programme, the service in practice fairly matches the stated concept of balance, and that, in a medium which has much to learn, the quality of their productions, though it can often be better, is generally good.

Appraisal of the BBC's television service: a summing up

148. We have now to summarize the conclusions we have reached on the conduct by the BBC of their service of television. Our clear impression is that the BBC's stated views on the purposes which the service should fulfil accord with those we have formulated earlier in the Report. The Corporation's traditional idea of public service remains the essential consideration in the formulation of policy. We are impressed by the BBC's awareness of the nature, the magnitude and the complexity of the task of catering for the needs of the public. It is easy to assert an awareness of principles, but the BBC appear also to have a grasp of their practical implications. In short, we found in the BBC an all-round *professionalism*. By this we mean not so much that there is at the

production level a competence, a mastery of present techniques. We mean that there is, at the executive levels where both principles and the public interest are interpreted and re-interpreted, a recognition of what—in terms of programme planning and performance—is needed to give substance to principles. This professionalism of the BBC shows itself not least in their dissatisfaction with performance, in their sense of the unrealized possibilities of the medium.

149. The BBC know good broadcasting; by and large, they are providing it. We set out to consider how far the main causes of disquiet and dissatisfaction were attributable to the BBC's television service. The BBC are not blameless; but the causes are not, we find, to any great extent attributable to their service. This is the broad consensus of view revealed by the representations put to us by people and organizations which spoke to us as viewers. Their view is perhaps seen most significantly in this; that whatever criticism they made of television, they nearly all went on to say that, if there were to be an additional television programme, it should be provided by the BBC. We have no hesitation in saying that the BBC command public confidence. If this is a test of the discharge of a public trust, then the BBC pass it. There are blemishes, too; mistakes, as there must be, of judgment. And we repeat that there was criticism of a more general kind which, we felt, had some substance; that the BBC had lowered their standards in some measure in order to compete with independent television. But our broad conclusion is this; that, within the limits imposed by a single programme, the BBC's television service is a successful realization of the purposes of broadcasting as defined in the Charter.

(iv) *A general appraisal of the independent television service*

156. The Authority was disposed to regard as exaggerated the commonly held view that television exerted a high degree of influence. That it would be a main factor in shaping the values and moral attitudes of our society in the next decades was, in Sir Ivone Kirkpatrick's submission, an over-simplification. He thought society would be largely what it was—with or without television. He would hesitate to accept a dictum that society was going to be in any way moulded by it. But he later agreed that television would be one of the influences moulding society, and that it might be more significant than any of the others. Though it could help to bring about the kind of society everyone would wish to see, it could not be put to this use by prescription.

90

157. The Authority's assessment óf the power of television differs greatly from that generally put to us by a wide variety of persons and organizations representative of the whole of our society, and from that suggested by such objective evidence as is available. These assessments rated the likely influence as profound.

158. The Authority therefore rated the responsibility of the broadcaster lower than did others who gave us their views. In fact, the Authority told us that, though there was a duty to widen tastes and affirm standards, the broadcaster's task was essentially to mirror society and its tastes as they are. This was what independent television had done, the Authority agreed, and it was difficult to see how it could have done more.

159. Nothing the Authority said to us suggested that, in its view, an essentially passive reflection of society would, by reinforcing existing assumptions and attitudes, itself affect society. Since the broadcaster's responsibility, as seen by the Authority, was essentially to ensure that television reflected society and its tastes as they are, it was not so much for him to ask: 'What is television doing to society?'—for the question would imply a responsibility of a different and more positive kind. The Authority's attitude was rather: 'This is what society is making of television.' In making these comments, we appreciate that the Authority's analogy—the mirror held up to society as it is—must not be taken absolutely, if only because the Authority is specifically obliged, for example, not to permit its service to offend public feeling, or to incite to crime. Nevertheless, as the Authority described it to us, the responsibility of the broadcaster is primarily and necessarily passive.

160. We were disturbed by these views. For the Authority so greatly to discount the effect of the medium and hence the nature of their responsibilities, seemed to us to be at variance with general opinion. And it runs counter to the evidence submitted to us by a wide variety of persons and representative organizations. Moreover, we have already concluded that, unless and until there is convincing proof to the contrary, the working assumption must remain that television will be a considerable factor in influencing values and moral standards. The Authority's working assumption is that television has little effect. This is, in our view, a mistake.

169. Though the Standing Consultative Committee's conclusion gave little indication of the Authority's views on the portrayal of violence, they are on record elsewhere. The Authority's views on the analysis published by the Council for Children's Welfare were given in a speech made by Sir Robert Fraser on 7th

November, 1960, when the Authority published their Report for 1959–60; copies of this speech were sent to us. Sir Robert pointed out that dramatists and story tellers had always taken crime and violence as their themes. He cited, in particular, the epics and drama of classical Greece, and Shakespearean tragedies and histories. The test was not, therefore, whether a play or story contained violence; it was rather its values—the moral values implicit in its presentation. Particular classes of programme must not therefore be dismissed en bloc; each programme must be examined on its merits and one must ask if there was humanity in it.

170. The Authority's view seems to be that since violence appears in great art (the classical Greek drama, Elizabethan drama, the novel) and is acceptable there, so must it be as acceptable in the Westerns and crime serials on television. It is true that the criteria applied to both should, in this respect, be roughly the same. But it is precisely when one invokes these criteria that television productions so often fail—for the basic test is: how far is the violence an integral, a necessary, part of the work of art: is it in any degree too much insisted on, used to produce sensation for its own sake? There is a further point. Much of the criticism of the portayal of violence was directed at its volume and incidence. It was, indeed, with the amount of violence on television, especially when children were watching, that the Council for Children's Welfare was primarily concerned. This criticism is not touched upon in Sir Robert's speech. And, of course, Shakespearean and classical Greek tragedy are not watched night after night on television.

171. This was not, however, the whole of the Authority's opinion. Giving oral evidence, Sir Ivone Kirkpatrick also referred to violence in Shakespeare and said that anything reflecting life must reflect violence. But he added that the portrayal of violence was objectionable if it was out of balance, or placed in a wrong context: it might be objectionable to show to children what it was proper to show to adults. More generally, he agreed that there was danger in constant repetition.

174. We conclude that the portrayal of violence, in its amount, treatment and timing, is unsatisfactory on independent television. Further, we believe that the Authority's policy on the portrayal of violence in television is defective on a number of counts. Generally it depends too much on the view that violence is part of life and must therefore be mirrored. There is validity in this view, but, unless it is supported by those further considerations about the

use of violence which we have noted above, it can easily become an excuse for the portrayal of too much violence for its own sake, rather than a justification for the portrayal of those incidents of violence that are properly part of an imaginatitive work. In particular, we consider that the Authority cannot, by relying on the policies towards violence of the individual companies, properly discharge its responsibilities. The policy should be prescribed by the Authority and not left to more than a dozen different companies. We recall the statement in the 1953 White Paper (Cmd. 9005) to the effect that it was the public corporation, free from the risk of outside pressure, which would be responsible for the standard of programmes. No code or stated policy could be perfect. But to exercise its responsibilities, the Authority should at least define the elements of a policy on violence. Further, the Authority should adopt the concept of family viewing time as this is normally understood: that is to say, that the general run of programmes up till a suitable break not earlier than 9 p.m. should be not unsuitable for children. To draw the line at 7 p.m. is to draw it too early; and it is not enough to prescribe that, thereafter, programmes should be graduated.

187. The main cause of dissatisfaction was, we noted, that the range of subject matter provided was insufficient to meet the wide variety of viewers' interests. We now note that it attaches very largely to the programmes of independent television. The TUC told us that independent television ignored the special interests of sections of the total audience. The Radio and Television Safeguards Committee, representing sixteen organizations whose members are wholly or partially occupied in broadcasting, suggested a failure of independent television to cater, except in a token manner, for any but the mass audience. The Society for Education in Film and Television said that independent television did not provide a balanced programme; there was a very low proportion of topical, documentary and educational items. There was dissatisfaction not only with the large quantity of mass-appeal items, but also with their timing. The National Union of Teachers and the TUC complained that independent television's serious programmes were mainly presented in off-peak hours. The Association of Education Committees told us that independent television under-estimated the public, and put on nearly all its better programmes late at night. The facts support these criticisms. We have recorded on page 89 the BBC's assessment of the percentage of peak viewing hours its service devotes to serious programmes. We asked the ITA to make an assessment for its

service. Again, the following kinds of programme were classed as serious: news and current affairs, talks and discussions, documentary programmes, outside broadcasts of national importance and other major events of a non-sporting character, music other than 'light music', ballet and opera, and religious broadcasts. These categories include all the kinds of programme—other than schools' programmes—listed by the Authority in the review paper submitted to us on 'The Serious Side of Independent Television'. There is, we realize, a measure of subjective judgment in allocating programmes to this or that class, but the proper classification of nearly all programmes is obvious enough. The following table gives the Authority's assessment.

Percentage of Hours given to Serious Programmes (excluding Drama) in the Independent Television Programme

	7–10.30 p.m.	All hours	Schools
January–June 1958	9	$17\frac{1}{4}$	$4\frac{1}{2}$
July–December 1958	$12\frac{3}{4}$	$16\frac{3}{4}$	$3\frac{1}{2}$
January–June 1959	$11\frac{1}{2}$	$17\frac{3}{4}$	5
July–December 1959	$15\frac{1}{2}$	$18\frac{1}{4}$	4
January–June 1960	$9\frac{1}{2}$	$16\frac{1}{2}$	$5\frac{1}{2}$
July–December 1960	$9\frac{1}{4}$	$19\frac{1}{2}$	3

It is evident that the time devoted by independent television to serious programmes is much less than that devoted to them by the BBC, both throughout the day and during the peak viewing period.

188. Both the Authority and the companies agreed that the amount and timing of serious programmes was deliberate. But they gave different reasons.

189. On the amount of serious programmes, the Authority told us that they were satisfied that the balance on independent television between the various classes of programme items was broadly right. Later, in a statement published on 1st February, 1962, the Director General said that the Authority was in no doubt that the requirement of the Television Act in the matter of balance was properly fulfilled. He said, also, of serious programmes, that there was more than enough to satisfy a viewer with no interest in entertainment programmes at all. The Authority's views on their criteria for deciding whether balance is right are given in two pages in their 1959–60 Report. On page 15, the Authority said:

The broad pattern of programmes during the year seemed to the Authority to be reasonably satisfactory in its balance. Not all programmes can be good in any television service, and those that will please many viewers will not please all. Perhaps the most important aims are to try to secure a continuously improving standard in popular programmes, while ensuring that there is much to appeal to the discriminating viewer who looks to television for more than entertainment.

On page 26, we read:

Again there are wide differences of opinion about what should constitute a 'proper balance in subject-matter' and a 'high general standard of quality'. In deciding on these matters, there is need for a responsible yet tolerant understanding of what constitutes public taste. Clearly a minority of highly educated viewers is likely to find unexacting and therefore uninteresting some programmes which severely test the comprehension of many of their fellows. Similarly, to those not otherwise predisposed to appreciate, say, ballet, classical music and serious drama on the one hand and 'rock'n roll' and simple quiz games on the other, such programmes will be devoid of interest and appeal. Both light and serious programmes should, however, always aim to be qualitatively as good as possible in their respective ways, and in the disposition of the programme time among the various categories of programmes those responsible for programme planning must strike the right balance between catering for the existing tastes of viewers and challenging their capacity to develop new ones.

190. We make four comments. First, the Authority believe that the service they are responsible for strikes the right balance. Those who have written to us as viewers believe that it has not. Second, the Authority state that a decision on balance must be based on a responsible yet tolerant understanding of what constitutes public taste, and they are satisfied that in this sense theirs is a good television service. This implies that the Authority recognize that they must try to assess the public's capacity for interest and enjoyment, and claim that they have succeeded in assessing it. But the representations put to us maintain that independent television has much under-estimated the public's capacity for interest and enjoyment. Third, the statement does not seem to recognize that we are all, as individuals, members sometimes of 'majority' and sometimes 'minority' audiences. Fourth, the Authority do not seem to regard it as a factor of importance that a person can watch different programmes with differing degrees of enjoyment, and is often more enthusiasic about the tastes and

interests he shares with minorities than those he shares with majorities.

191. The Authority told us that serious programmes were deliberately placed outside peak viewing hours. The aim was to get the maximum audience for them, and the best way to achieve this aim was by putting them on when it was unlikely that the BBC would be putting out a big entertainment. In the statement published on 7th November, 1960, Sir Robert Fraser justified their timing as follows: 'And could we perhaps hear the last of this criticism that they'—that is serious programmes—'are too late to matter? If we strike a balance of viewers' preferences, they are not ill-placed where they are. Their timing is deliberate and sensible: the proof of the pudding is in the eating. They enjoy very large audiences.' The Authority supported this argument by tables showing that independent television's programmes shown outside peak hours achieved higher ratings than did BBC programmes shown during peak hours.

192. We believe that this policy is open to the objection that many viewers find it impossible or inconvenient to watch outside peak hours—indeed it is for this reason that these hours are peak hours. As the Independent Group of Conservatives said: 'Catering for minorities does not mean always putting on minority taste programmes at times when the average viewer has not arrived home from work or is in bed.' For children, as several organizations pointed out, this is particularly important. Children's tastes and interests are formed by what they see far more than are those of adults; when children are viewing, the variety of programmes should be as wide as possible.

193. In the Authority's view, then, the present amount and timing of serious programmes reflects their deliberate policy. If this policy were the cause of present practice, we would say that it relied on a misinterpretation both of the nature of television's audience, and of the best way of satisfying its needs.

194. The evidence of many of the companies suggests another reason for the practice of independent television. All the main companies agreed that they had a responsibility for leading public taste, and that this implied a responsibility to cater for 'minority' as well as 'majority' tastes. But whereas the Authority thought that the service now catered sufficiently for minorities, the companies on the whole did not. One reason was that there was not enough room within a single programme. But another was that, since independent television derived its revenue from advertising, it was bound to seek the largest audiences. Anglia Television

said that independent television must be concerned to hold the maximum audience; Associated Rediffusion said that it was inevitable that it should serve the majority; for Scottish Television, Mr Thomson said that, because advertisers paid for viewers, 'it is inevitable in the system that you should be reaching generally for a maximum'; for Southern Television, Mr Dowson said that it was 'impractical' to put out opera, because no advertiser would be prepared to buy advertising time knowing that the audience would be small. This was also one of the reasons for the placing of serious programmes outside peak hours. Associated Rediffusion in their written evidence agreed with the Authority; they said that the majority need inevitably had preference in peak hours, then added, to our surprise, 'it should not be assumed, however, that the most convenient and popular times for viewing on the part of minorities are the same as those for the majorities'. When they gave oral evidence, however, Sir Edwin Herbert told us that the BBC could and did put out more serious programmes in peak hours. For Southern Television, Mr Downson told us that the commercial element prevented the showing of minority programmes at peak hours. He agreed that this was wrong: it was for this reason that Southern Television suggested a limited form of sponsorship for such programmes.

195. We have, then, two explanations of the amount and timing of serious programmes in independent television: the Authority's —that it was considered policy; and the companies'—that it was commercially inevitable. By saying that some of the companies recognize these consequences of commercial considerations, we imply neither that all did, nor that they saw no other reason. But this explanation was put to us by some companies, and was widely believed to be true by many organizations which wrote to us as viewers or as performers.

196. The companies' evidence should not be taken as suggesting that advertisers have directly influenced the content of programmes. Only one specific allegation was made to us on that score. We were told that a programme for schools on advertising, one of a series dealing with the agencies of mass persuasion, was revised. The revision was contrary to the wishes of those who had designed the programme, so that its purpose—to teach awareness of the methods of mass persuasion—was frustrated. It was suggested that this revision was brought about by the intervention of advertising interests. After a lapse of years much of the evidence was obscure and we found it impossible to ascertain all the facts or to verify their sequence. Accordingly we pronounce no opinion

on this particular case but mention it as an illustration of the pressures that could arise from the conflicting interests present in independent television.

208. We conclude that the stated views of the Authority on the purposes of broadcasting do not accord with those we have formulated earlier in the Report. The differences are not only of emphasis. The role of the broadcasting organization, as the Authority interpreted it to us, seemed to lack that positive and active quality which is essential to good broadcasting. We reject, too, its view that television will be shaped by society. A number of factors will operate to shape television, to form the character of the service; but what must figure very largely are the attitudes, the convictions, the motives of those who provide programmes—who plan and produce what we see on our television screens. Their role is not passive; they in turn will be helping, however imperceptibly, to affect society.

209. The disquiet about and dissatisfaction with television are, in our view, justly attributed very largely to the service of independent television. This is so despite the popularity of the service, and the well-known fact that many of its programmes command the largest audiences. Our enquiries have brought us to appreciate why this kind of success is not the only, and is by no means the most important, test of a good broadcasting service. Indeed, it is a success which can be obtained by abandoning the main purposes of broadcasting. Just as significant a pointer to popular opinion is this: that of all those many organizations which spoke as viewers and have no other interest, none speaking from a consideration of the character of the service to be provided advocated that 'the third television programme' should be allotted to independent television; and those very few who did so explained that they were concerned to ensure that any new service would not be a direct charge to the public. Many indeed specifically urged that the service of independent television should on no account be extended. We conclude that the service of independent television does not successfully realize the purposes of broadcasting as defined in the Television Act.

210. As we said earlier, it is the Authority that is the answerable public corporation. But we would add that it has to contend with difficulties of a kind from which the BBC is free. The Authority does not engage in programme planning and production; it is regulatory, and operates at a remove from those whose function in television is positive, from those who plan and produce programmes. Though the policies of the Authority seem to us to be

at several important points misconceived, we became increasingly aware that this was not a complete explanation of the failings of independent television. It seemed as though the fault might be organic.

11 From: ITA Annual Report 1964-65

VIOLENCE IN PROGRAMMES

Independent Television Code

The Television Act 1964 required the Independent Television Authority to draw up, and from time to time review, a code giving guidance about the showing of scenes of violence, particularly when large numbers of children and young persons may be expected to be watching the programmes. The provisions of the code drawn up by the Authority and applied throughout Independent Television are as follows:

The Context of Violence

1. Conflict, the clash of purposes and personalities, is a major element in drama, and not least in great drama. Physical violence is conflict at the point when blows are exchanged or weapons are used. Persecution, bullying, intimidation, humiliation and cruelty are forms of mental violence, and it is well to remember that the suffering thus caused may exceed that caused by physical violence, though not a hand has been raised to strike.

2. The first rule in the control of both forms of violence must always be to examine the dramatic context in which they occur, and the ends to which they are a means. For, if need be, physical force may be used to protect the law as well as break it, to defend the guiltless or helpless as well as oppress them, to impose a just settlement as well as an unjust one, and anger may take the form of a just moral indignation against the infliction of cruelty, as well as of a vicious outburst of temper or a mercilessly sustained vendetta.

3. Therefore, in dramatic programmes likely to be seen by children, the initial question to be asked is whether they are

pervaded with a clear sense of right and wrong. All may turn on the answer. For children acquire their moral sentiments from the society around them, including its aspect in television, and particularly from those they admire both in real life and in literature and drama. They tend to model their own conduct on the conduct of those they admire, and shun the conduct of those they feel to be bad. It follows that the ends for which characters presented to them as admirable resort to physical force should always be socially defensible.

Violence for its own sake not permissible

4. The second rule, which follows from the first, is that violence, whether physical or mental, should never be allowed 'for its own sake'—that is to say, simply because it attracts or secures the attention of audiences, or certain types of audience. If the nature of it, or the sheer quantity of it, goes beyond its dramatic function, it should be cut. Individual brutality or the aimless violence of mobs can be shown; but there comes a point at which they have exhausted their dramatic role—and at that point they should stop. Purely quantitative control is important.

Intensity of Violence

5. The third rule concerns the quality or intensity of violence. This may be a question of distance or closeness in space and time. A long shot of an ambush or cavalry charge is one thing; a close-up of facial agony, though part of that whole, is another. Distance in time, the remoteness of the setting from our world, may also lessen the emotional impact of violence. The senses are less vividly impressed. It may also be lessened when the story is simply not regarded as real—the fairy story, the conventional adventure story or the re-created world of the routine Western, with its stock characters, or the puppet, marionette, and mime. But not too much importance should be attached to this form of 'distance'. Reality can shrink distance, and thrust through any convention. Horror in costume is still horror.

The Protection of Children

6. Within this broad frame of reference, great care should always be taken in the presentation of the following:

(a) *Scenes likely to frighten children*

There are degrees of fear, from the mild and half-pleasurable fear of climbing a tree or a mountain to absolute unmixed terror, and children vary greatly in their susceptibility to

100

fear. Horror deliberately presented as an entertainment should be prohibited.

(b) *Scenes likely to unnerve and unsettle children*
Care must be taken to guard children against the impression that they are entering a world in which they can count on nothing as settled, reliable and kind, and in which they must make their way at the expense of others, resorting to physical or mental violence whenever it will pay them.

(c) *Scenes likely to cause pain to children*
Pain witnessed, except by a brute, is pain felt. When witnessed the pain of others stirs sympathy, and the desire arises to relieve suffering, and protect the weak or helpless against it. This is a stage of moral growth. But there are degrees of suffering altogether too painful for children to watch. The more helpless the victim, such as the aged, the infirm, or an animal, the greater the pain induced in a good-hearted child.

(d) *Scenes in which pleasure is taken in the infliction of pain or humiliation upon others*
Children should know that bullies are a fact of life, but great care must be taken to see that they despise them and do not secretly admire them. When such scenes reach the level of deliberate torture, they should be either momentary or banned entirely.

(e) *Scenes in which the infliction or acceptance of pain or humiliation is associated with sexual pleasure*
These should be eliminated.

(f) *Scenes which children might copy with injury to themselves or others*
Children are imitative and curious. The technique of hanging, or experiments with fire, or tying and locking up, or submerging in water, can easily be tried by a child.

(g) *Scenes in which easily acquired and dangerous weapons are used*
It is a simple fact that guns and swords are not easily come by, while knives, bottles, bars and bricks are. It is not good that children with a tendency to violence should see them in frequent use.

(h) *Scenes in which the less usual methods of inflicting injury are employed*
This includes rabbit punches, suffocation, the sabotage of vehicles, and dangerous booby traps.

7. In cases of doubt, cut. The risk is not one that can decently be taken.

12 From: Report of the Committee on Broadcasting 1960

A CODE OF PRACTICE FOR THE B.B.C. TELEVISION SERVICE

A note by Controller of Programmes, Television

Introduction

It is recognized that it is difficult and undesirable to be dogmatic about a subject which has a great many and diverse aspects; the type of programme, the time of its showing and the likely composition of the audience for whom it is intended are three of the major considerations which will condition the decisions taken by producers, output heads and others responsible for what appears on the screen. To attempt to lay down laws too precisely to meet all situations would be to invite inconsistency. Nevertheless, there are certain lines of thought, certain current practices, and an accumulation of experience, which in effect constitute a policy. it is a policy which is carried out empirically, perhaps even instinctively, and that is hazardous.

There is no reason why the main principles on which decisions are based should not be the same, and be applied in the same way, whether the programme is a studio drama or a hired telefilm, a magazine item or a documentary, part of children's television or part of that area of adult time when children are known to be viewing in substantial numbers. To talk of good taste, commonsense and the avoidance of extremes is not enough. An attempt to lay down a general code of practice may be of positive value in ensuring that in avoiding harm on the one hand, we do not impoverish or emasculate our material on the other.

Children's Programmes

(The following points are of importance also to all those concerned with programmes up to 9 p.m.):

(1) The worlds which children and grown-ups occupy, though they overlap, are different. Subjects with unpleasant associations for the one will often be taken for granted by the other. Guns and fisticuffs may have sinister implications for adults; seldom for children. Family insecurity and marital infidelity may be commonplace to adults; to children they can be deeply disturbing.

(2) A black-list is therefore impracticable. Torture is normally inadmissible, yet in 'Jesus of Nazareth' the Crucifixion was dramatized. In a particular context, many subjects which would at first sight seem wrong for children's viewing, can be justified. But danger-points can be stressed, especially for those engaged in drama and in the selection of films.

(3) These are the main danger points:

(a) Situations which upset a child's emotional security, arising out of adoption, desertion, cruelty in the home, unwanted children, friction between parents, especially in contemporary settings. H.C.P. Tel. well says of these: 'Perhaps not violence, but violation, which is worse.'

(b) Portrayal of injury, illness or disablements, especially when used to sharpen a dramatic crisis (e.g. nightmares); and of embarrassing personal disabilities (e.g. stuttering).

(c) Dangerous examples of 'villainous' action which invite imitation, e.g. the use of intriguing weapons, traps and pitfalls, from sabotaged bicycles to trip-wires.

(d) Bad habits in 'good' characters; e.g. chain-smoking, hitting below the belt.

(e) Brutality: the most difficult category. Brutality is not the same thing as violence. Violence is not the same thing as combat. Yet because combat, which is healthy, and brutality, which is not, both contain violence, they tend to become identified. Over-emphasis in picture and sound is one key. Long-shot renders many affrays and battles inoffensive; close-up makes the same incidents inadmissible.

(f) Weapons: the choice is important. Coshes, knives, whips and bottles are more suspect than revolvers, rifles or swords, because they are more easily available or improvised.

(g) Atmosphere: This can be more upsetting than violence because here what is essentially a subjective subject

103

becomes most personal. To chill the spine is a legitimate part of story-telling. To create an eerie and fearful atmosphere, especially with the aid of background music, or sudden optical shock, can be more than momentarily disturbing. The supernatural, especially in modern dress, is perilous ground.

(4) Commonsense, though it may not be enough, nevertheless demands that stories must have conflict, that if there are to be heroes, there must be villains also, that escapism is an inadequate basis for planning, and that risks must sometimes be run if the wholesome appetite of children for excitement and for getting to grips with life is to be satisfied.

Adult Programmes

These may be divided into two categories, first, documentary and magazine programmes containing film sequences of actual happenings, and, second, dramatic programmes, whether in the studio or on film, where the scenes have been deliberately contrived.

(1) Producers with library material to draw upon must always satisfy themselves first of all that the illustrations they choose which depict scenes of violence, brutality or horror are valid and essential to their theme, that the meaning of the programme is, indeed, heightened by the inclusion of such sequences. They must then ask themselves if the effect of including those scenes is not, in the case of a large number of normal viewers, going to cause such distress or resentment as to invalidate the programme altogether for those people. If we expose viewers to shock, or indeed to fear, we must be absolutely certain in advance that our reasons are good and proper ones. They may well be, but justification by hindsight is not acceptable.

(2) Scenes of physical violence are an almost invariable ingredient of all American importations other than comedy or musical shows. They often occur, though customarily in less extended or extreme form, in our own plays and serials. While it is axiomatic that we do not permit, either on telecine or in the studio, the gratuitous exploitation of violence as a source of unwholesome entertainment, there are certain principles which should be common to all concerned and which may be usefully restated.

(a) A sequence involving violence should arise naturally from the story, and be therefore dramatically necessary and defensible. If it is inserted extraneously for depraved effect, it should be rejected outright. This happens with many of the 'private eye' and police series which come from the United States. The 'western', on the other hand, has a formal and stylized tradition, of which shooting and slogging it out are an essential part. The latest film-makers, however, are apt to interject a sudden piece of optical or acoustic self-indulgence into an otherwise admissible fight between law and outlaw. This requires vigilance from us.

(b) Any such 'natural' sequence should not be unduly prolonged.

(c) No sequence should include shots which dwell upon the more gruesome and bloody physical aspects of a combat.

(d) As with children's programmes, the use of dangerous implements, other than firearms, has to be watched, to avoid both revulsion and imitation in viewers.

(g) Sound effects and sound track should not distort or magnify the impact of violence, e.g. the breaking of bones, the cracking of skull or jaw.

(f) In a fist fight, neither contestant should engage in tactics of a vicious or bestial nature.

(g) Violence inflicted on a woman or animal must require special scrutiny.

If there is any suspicion that a scene has been written, or filmed, deliberately to scare the imaginative and/or nervous viewer, then it should automatically be excised.

Equally important, consideration should be given to the concept of the film or play, to the purpose and intentions of the producer or author and the means they have employed to carry those out. We must not carelessly dismiss their integrity.

Finally, the most important rule for all staff is to refer for further examination anything about which they are doubtful. The effect of such reference in the long run is much more likely to be positive than negative. Responsibility shared means progress, not regression.

KENNETH ADAM

7th March, 1960

13   From: ITV 1970, A guide to Independent Television

The ITV Audience

Audience Size and Composition

Information on the size and composition of the audience is provided for ITV by an independent research organization, Audits of Great Britain Ltd (AGB), through JICTAR, the Joint Industry Committee for Television Advertising Research, which is responsible for the service. A full description of the way in which audience measurement is undertaken is given on pages 108–111.

About 51 million people in over $16\frac{1}{2}$ million homes have television sets able to receive Independent Television programmes. This coverage amounts to 95 per cent of the total population. From January to July 1969, in homes which could receive both BBC and Independent Television, the set was switched on for an average of 4·5 hours per day; for 2·4 hours it was tuned to Independent Television and for 2·1 hours to BBC. Audiences for the most popular programmes exceeded twenty million viewers.

Audiences for Different Types of Programmes

The size of the audience for different television programmes varies considerably. Apart from the general popularity or quality of a programme, the number of people viewing it is affected by many different factors, such as the day and time of transmission, the programmes before and after and the attractiveness of the programmes available on the other channels. Also, because of regional variations in the programme schedules of the different Independent Television areas, a number of programmes which are highly popular in the areas in which they are shown fail to appear among the list of those seen by the largest number of viewers over the country as a whole. The table on page 109 shows the twenty programmes on Independent Television and the BBC television services which were seen in the largest numbers of viewing homes during a typical week in September 1969.

Audience Research

Measurement of the size and composition of the audience for programmes, although an essential component of audience re-

106

search, does not by itself provide sufficient information in order adequately to understand public reactions to programmes. The Authority has, therefore, continued to supplement audience measurement data with other research data derived from various sources, and has laid the foundations for a comprehensive audience reaction service. This is being undertaken, in the first place, on a limited pilot basis jointly with the programme companies, starting in the Autumn of 1969. This pilot research is confined to three areas—London, Lancashire and Central Scotland—and limited to six months' duration. The decision on the scope and form of the main reaction service for Independent Television will be based upon the lessons learnt during this pilot operation.

Samples of 300 viewers, selected by strictly statistical methods to be representative of the audience in each area, will return completed questionnaires to the independent research organization (Television Opinion Panel Ltd or TOP) which is responsible for the project. This information will provide the basis for regular reports to the ITA and all programme companies on the degree of enjoyment or appreciation of all programmes seen. In addition a series of evaluations will be made of a selection of programmes, showing not only the ways in which the viewers are reacting to the programmes, but the ways in which the programmes are thought to differ from other programmes of a similar kind.

The research undertaken for the ITA consultation on religious television at Canterbury in 1968, in which the attitudes, values and beliefs of the British public were investigated, aroused considerable interest in Northern Ireland. The original survey did not include Ulster, and it was felt that the different situation there merited special consideration. The research was, therefore, repeated in Northern Ireland, jointly financed and sponsored by a committee of all the Churches in Northern Ireland, Ulster Television and the ITA. In addition to the questions asked in Great Britain, some special questions relating to the situation in Ulster were included. A pamphlet summarizing the results of the survey was subsequently published by Ulster Television.

The Authority has continued to undertake regular public opinion surveys, designed to provide information about general public attitudes to the Independent Television programme output. The Authority has also continued with its basic research programme, which is concerned with the determination and measurement of factors affecting the pattern of viewing of the audience. Viewers' satisfaction depends on the selection of programmes chosen from the available output on all channels, and the ways in which this selection is made provide indications of the optimum balance of programmes from the viewer's own standpoint. In this basic research, a thorough and systematic analysis of audience measurement data is undertaken in order to find out the importance of various scheduling and programme factors in shaping the decisions of the viewer in the formation of his choice of viewing pattern.

A special research project has been commissioned with the aim of finding out the characteristics and viewing preferences of the actual and potential audience during the afternoon period from midday until 6 p.m. Particular attention is being paid to the presence and preferences of special minority sections of the public—shift workers, mothers of pre-school age children, old people, etc. The results will provide valuable guidance in the construction of afternoon programme schedules designed to meet special needs within the context of a balanced total output.

Measuring the Audience
Meeting the needs of the programme planners, as well as the buyers and sellers of television advertising time, in measuring the viewing behaviour of some seventeen million family audiences is the industry body known as JICTAR. JICTAR (the Joint Industry Committee for Television Advertising Research) represents three bodies: the Incorporated Society of British Advertisers Ltd (ISBA), the Institute of Practitioners in Advertising (IPA), and the Independent Television Companies' Association Ltd (ITCA). Since 30 July 1968, when the new programme contracts came into force, the research data for JICTAR have been prepared by Audits of Great Britain Ltd (AGB) at Audit House, the research centre at Eastcote, Middlesex.

The service is based upon panels which are representative of ITV homes in each of the areas defined on the BBTA (British Bureau of Television Advertising) regional maps. These panels are selected, maintained and revised on the basis of large 'random sample' establishment surveys carried out in each area each year. Panel selection is determined by television reception characteristics, geographical location, demographic features and the predicted weight of viewing. In the London area alone, the viewing characteristics of some 350 households, representing 990 individuals, are measured on a minute-by-minute basis, while on a national scale (excluding the Channel Islands) the panel comprises 2,650 households and 7,790 individuals.

Network Top Twenty
Week ended 14th September 1969

Programme	Originator	Homes viewing
Who-Dun-it	ATV	7·35 millions
The Best Things in Life	ATV	6·95 millions
Public Eye	Thames	6·65 millions
News at Ten (Wednesday)	ITN	6·65 millions
News at Ten (Tuesday)	ITN	6·30 millions
Coronation Street (Monday)	Granada	6·25 millions
Coronation Street (Wednesday)	Granada	5·90 millions
Never Mind the Quality, Feel the Width	Thames	5·90 millions
You've Made Your Bed, Now Lie In It	Anglia	5·70 millions
News at Ten (Thursday)	ITN	5·65 millions
World in Action	Granada	5·60 millions
Doctor in the House	London Weekend	5·60 millions
News at Ten (Monday)	ITN	5·50 millions
Softly, Softly	BBC	5·50 millions
Not in Front of the Children	BBC	5·35 millions
The Jimmy Tarbuck Show	ATV	5·30 millions
Opportunity Knocks!	Thames	5·25 millions
This Week	Thames	5·20 millions
Dick Van Dyke	BBC	5·20 millions
Dad's Army	BBC	5.15 millions
Wojeck	BBC	5·15 millions
The Frankie Howerd Show	ATV	5·15 millions

© JICTAR 1969

The Information

For the greatest possible accuracy, some six different types of information have to be merged to produce the weekly reports for subscribers. These are:

1 The statistics and characteristics of each household, recorded on a master file.

2 The amount of viewing, and to which channel, in every home as recorded on the SETmeter, the sophisticated electronic device developed by AGB.

3 A record of who in each family is watching and when, determined by SET diaries, submitted each week by the housewife.

4 A post-transmission programme log from each of the ITV companies and the BBC to determine the exact timing of the programme schedule transmitted each day.

5 A commercial log from each of the ITV companies giving the time and nature of every commercial transmitted.

6 A report of the current advertising rates in force at the time of transmission of each commercial.

109

Process

At Audit House, the week runs from Monday to Sunday and the whole process of audience measurement starts on Monday morning when the housewife recovers the tape from the SETmeter and, together with the individual viewing diaries, posts it to AGB. Ninety per cent arrive safely by Tuesday morning, when the work of sorting the tapes and viewing diaries begins and the information is booked in by a cardex system. The next stage in the operation is to translate the information on the tape into special punched paper tape capable of being read by the computer, a Honeywell 1200. This is done on an 'encoder'.

The viewing diaries, completed on a quarter-hour basis by each member of the household panel and any guests, are similarly transferred on punched paper tape by means of a 'Lector'. Information from the programme logs of each of the ITV companies is then coded and put on to punched cards.

By Wednesday night, all of the requisite information is available in a form suitable for the computer to digest and the process of feeding the Honeywell commences.

Thursday morning sees the computer drawing graphs, by means of an attachment called 'Calcomp', of the minute-by-minute audience levels to ITV and BBC for each day for each ITV region. The computer also produces columns of viewing and cost information and these 'print-outs' are pasted-up, checked and photographed before being printed on one of the eight 'Multilith' machines at Audit House.

The last stage in the process is the collating and packing of individual reports prior to despatching them to subscribers on the Friday evening.

JICTAR and the BBC

The audience share figures quoted by AGB on behalf of JICTAR and the figures quoted by the BBC's Audience Research Department are often dissimilar and apparently incompatible. Confusion arises from the fact that both sets of findings are expressed simply as 'percentage audience shares' and, in consequence, are taken to be widely differing answers to the same question. In reality, both organizations are providing answers to two differing questions. The BBC provides 'percentage audience shares' in terms of the average individual, whilst AGB provides 'percentage audience shares' in terms of the average household's viewing.

Further, the JICTAR sample is confined to households with multi-channel receivers and excludes those households which are

110

considered to be incapable of receiving ITV programmes reliably, whereas the BBC embraces the whole population (excluding children under five), admitting anyone whether he has an ITV/ BBC television set, a BBC only television set, or neither.

Finally, JICTAR figures are based on minute-by-minute meter readings over the total transmission time, whereas BBC figures are limited to 47 hours of joint viewing time each week and are based on interviews made the day after the broadcast.

14 From: Television and The Child by H. T. Himmelweit, A. N. Oppenheim and Pamela Vance

Violence in Westerns and Detective Crime Plays

The following devices were used in children's Westerns to take the edge off violence:

Stylized presentation. Menace, attack, and injury are, like the characters, presented in a stylized manner. Tight lips and steely eyes convey menace. There is a limited and stereotyped range of traditional responses to injury; injury from behind is indicated by throwing back the shoulders, jerking up the head, and tumbling to the ground; a shot from the front is conveyed by clutching the stomach.

The camera veers away from the dead—it shows the leap, stagger, or fall that precedes death, but moves at once from the inert body.[1] Interest, in fact, is centred on the group, not on the unfortunate individual. Wounds are never defined and never cause serious disfigurement.

Stereotyped use of guns. At the centre of the preoccupation with violence is the gun. Everyone has a gun ready for immediate use— even the barbers and storekeepers, who are not cowboys. People in Westerns take guns for granted. It would be impossible to learn

[1] In the films viewed, there was only one death-scene and then only because the dying man had to give vital information.

anything from a Western about real guns and how they work. What is more, guns are generally ineffective; in one fairly typical Western we found that 149 shots were fired, yet no one was killed and only one man seriously injured, a second one slightly. Even when lethal, guns are aimed at a distance.

Finally, while guns are used mostly for fighting, they are also let off for fun. Nevertheless, guns spell power, they make people listen, and force them to do what is wanted.

Frequency of aggression by good and bad people. Villains use verbal threats more but, when it comes to real fighting by fist or gun, they wound and kill fewer people than the other side does. In fact, if good is to triumph, good people must successfully kill or wound. This may worry humane persons; for children it has less significance because the hero with whom they identify themselves is never in doubt about what to do, never sentimentalizes over his victims, and never pays for victory. He is not even personally involved in the kill, since it is rarely his gun or his fist which wounds the villain, however much he has done to bring it about. Table 30 gives the incidence of acts of violence perpetrated by the hero's and the villain's side respectively.

TABLE 30. Incidence of threats and acts of violence in eight Westerns on children's television

	Number of occasions	
	Hero's side	Villain's side
Verbal threats or abuse . .	4	10
Seizure by arms . . .	1	2
Fisticuffs	6	6
Shooting matches . . .	9	9
Wounding	3	1
Killing	3	2
Total	26	30

NOTE. Each act of violence consists here of very many individual incidents. One shooting match may involve several people and fifty or more gun shots.

Disguise of violence with humour. While children's Westerns pass lightly over death they dwell on and emphasize the earlier stages of violence for their entertainment value. Here are two examples from different films:

1. Hero and henchman go to a shack where dangerous villains are hiding. A fight ensues in which the henchman, with his back to the wall, is repeatedly punched on the chin, falling back under each blow. During the fight this vignette is

reproduced no less than four times—each time the situation was exactly the same. (This is where the humour of the situation is supposed to tell.) The henchman is being punched senseless, without mercy, against the back wall of the shack. Each time his expression is exaggeratedly foolish (meant to provoke laughter) and he is hardly conscious. The villain punching him never slackens or stops. The henchman re-appears later as right as rain.

2. This time the henchman is delivering the blows. It is precisely the same humorous situation, a little refined. The victim is propped up against the bar in a saloon. He is punched time and again with energy and precision, but as he leans against the bar he cannot fall down. At last the henchman stops, not for mercy, but to ask the hero why this cross-eyed unconscious man does not fall down. 'Try moving him away from the bar' the hero suggests. The already senseless man is stood away from the bar, punched again on the jaw, and collapses out of sight. With a smile the henchman turns to the hero for praise.

The humour of all this lies in the foolish expression of the victim, the regular delivery of punches, and the satisfaction shown by the aggressor. The impression they give is of adults at play; but there is an underlying element of viciousness, since these episodes are frills, unnecessary for the development of the plot.

Use of tension. Tension is created by the promise of more violence and conveyed by silence and slow and stealthy movement. It is relieved by the sight and sound of horses galloping. The object is to make the viewer believe that this time the hero is in such danger that he cannot get away unharmed. There is usually one such scene in each episode.

In general, then, violence in Westerns is abstract, stylized, and made readily acceptable because the hero never hesitates to apply it and none of its moral consequences are ever dwelt on. Despite moments of tension, violence is disguised to look remote and inconsequential—in fact, a game.

. . .

Violence

It is in the handling of violence, however, that these programmes[1] differ most from children's Westerns and from one another. In detective and crime plays, violence is made to look realistic and personal. It is not conventionalized.

[1] Detective and crime plays, analysed in the passage omitted.

First, there is no attempt to evade the consequences of violence, the camera stays with a man who has been hit; we see blood on his hands and beads of sweat on his face; we hear him gasp for air. *Dragnet* shows detailed expressions of physical pain, expressions which vary from one incident to another. The camera, the music, the effects all underline the realism. The viewer is in no way helped to believe that what he sees is only part of a story.

In Westerns the impact of violence is dulled because there are no close-ups at the kill and also because the emphasis is on opposing sides, rather than on individuals. In *Dragnet*, violence becomes a personal thing—and whenever a gun is fired, a knife aimed, or a fist shot out, it is always effective. In two out of the four *Dragnet* episodes there were incidents of vicious violence and gratuitous horrors.[1]

Violence in *Dragnet* is there to create sensation; it does not further the plot. In each of the episodes of *Inner Sanctum* there is at least one incident of excessive violence.

The episodes of *Fabian* that we monitored contain no murders, those of *Dragnet* two, and of *Inner Sanctum* three. Similarly, *Fabian* has on average four, *Dragnet* five, and *Inner Sanctum* six incidents of violence in one programme. The nature (as well as the amount) of violence is less serious in *Fabian* than in the other two.

Implications derived from the comparative analysis of children's Westerns, crime and detective programmes

The comparative analysis of children's Westerns, crime and detective series has brought out a number of points:

First, Westerns present a simple situation in which the permutations of plot, characterization, motives, and presentation of violence can readily be learned. On these grounds alone, we would expect children, once they have learned the choreography of the Westerns, to cease to be disturbed by the violence contained in them. On the other hand, the crime and detective programmes (which after all are designed for adults) are more difficult to predict; the motivation is more complex, the characterization less clear-cut. Particularly since the presentation of and the setting in which violence occurs varies from episode to episode, the format cannot readily be learned. This is especially true in crime thrillers like *Inner Sanctum*, where there is not even a central figure like a

---

[1] For instance, the ankles and arms of a dead girl in the *Big Trunk* were twice shown with the rope biting into her flesh, while in another episode there was a realistic close-up of a quivering lower arm, with blood running down it.

detective who recurs from episode to episode to provide the reassurance that comes with familiarity.

Second, Westerns are studies in black and white; crime and detective stories, studies in grey. In the Westerns, the villain has no identity; sympathy with his fate is not invited. This is not the case in crime and detective series where the complex motives of the villain are often expressed and with it sympathy for him invited. In this way a conflict of identification is set up in the child's mind and makes it more difficult for him to experience relief when the criminal is apprehended; in the case of children's Westerns this relief is complete.

Finally, the extent to which violence on television will prove disturbing to the child cannot be measured by the number of shots fired or the number of aggressive episodes contained in any one programme. It depends far more on the setting in which the violence occurs, on the manner of its presentation, and on the complexity of the characterization of the two sides in the struggle.

On all these counts, violence is seen as little disturbing for the child familiar with Westerns, but in the case of the crime and detective series the extent to which it arouses tension will depend on the particular manner in which the theme, characterization, and violence are handled in any given episode.

Passivity and Stimulation

Many parents and educationists in the United States expressed concern about the possibility that television might make children passive, usually in such broad terms as:

> I just think it's dangerous. Just sitting around having things thrown at you without stirring a muscle is very bad for children in my opinion.

The survey of teachers' opinions in this country showed that 25 per cent of them felt much the same and rated passivity second in the list of television's harmful effects. About 11 per cent referred to physical passivity—doing fewer things, being less active— and 14 per cent to mental passivity:

> It makes children less inclined to think for themselves, or to undertake creative activities.
> Children are less self-reliant; it induces a lazy attitude of mind.
> It dulls the imagination.

115

Such criticisms were made significantly more often by teachers who disapproved of television and by those who rarely viewed. It is possible, then, that the belief that television increases passivity is merely a convenient way of expressing prejudice against television; conversely, rejection of the belief may conveniently follow from personal acceptance and enjoyment of viewing. It seems unlikely that either group of teachers consistently had more 'passive' children in their classes than the other.

What do people mean by passivity?

Five aspects are frequently mentioned:
1. Viewing itself is a passive mental activity—the child sits immobile, open-mouthed, and drinks in all that the screen offers—he absorbs the content of television like a sponge.
2. Viewing may lead the child to prefer an edited version of life to life itself. At the turn of a knob, entertainment, interesting personalities, and events are brought effortlessly to the child. This becomes so satisfying that he acquires a taste for seeing things second-hand rather than making the effort to see (or do) the real thing for himself.
3. Viewing leads to 'spectatorism' and loss of initiative. This argument is really an extension of the one above. It suggests that when television is not available, the child will turn to other forms of spectator entertainment—the radio or the cinema—rather than engage in active play.
4. Television leads to a jaded palate. The child is being bombarded by a great diversity of stimuli; one or the other may interest him, but he will not translate it into action because immediately afterwards something else is offered which diverts his attention.
5. Viewing dulls the imagination. It provides the child with ready-made fantasy material so that he makes less use of his creative imaginative abilities.

There is a fear that a group of apathetic spectators will succeed the pre-television generation of alert, active 'doers'. It is worth recalling that anxieties about films and the radio were expressed in very similar terms. The criticism also equates physical inactivity with mental inactivity; and yet story-tellers and teachers know very well that children who sit still and listen spellbound are children who are responding intellectually and emotionally to what is being told. The mothers' diaries, too, show how a child

116

who is interested in a programme and likely to ask questions about it afterwards is just the one who sits enthralled and will not budge while the programme is on.

The criticisms examined

'*The child absorbs television like a sponge.*' This assertion can be readily dismissed in the light of our findings about the effects of television on values and outlook. There is no evidence whatever that viewing is of necessity a mentally passive affair. It is no more passive than watching a play in the theatre; it may be no more passive than reading a light book, once the process of reading has become automatic. But in both these instances the child or adult makes a choice; with television the choice is more limited and less physical exertion is needed.

'*Viewing leads the child to prefer an edited version of life to life itself.*' The evidence we gathered suggests that fears on this score are unnecessary. We devised a questionnaire entitled 'Ideas about TV' and asked the question: *Some people like to watch things and people on TV—others like to see the real thing for themselves. If you had the chance to see these people and places, how would you like to see them —in real life, or on TV?*

Twenty-seven places or personalities were listed and for each the child was asked to tick one of the following answers:

I would best like to see this on TV.
I would best like to see this for myself—the real thing.
I am not interested in seeing this at all.[1]

We chose six groups of subjects for examination, each representing some particular advantage that television might offer in relation to seeing the thing for oneself.[2] Items were only included when we felt confident that the children could have seen something of the sort on television and so would have a basis for making their choices.

The first two groups—ceremonial and sports events—are events where the screen affords a closer and more detailed view than would be possible if actually present. The ceremonial events chosen were: Trooping the Colour, the Lord Mayor's Show, and the Coronation Procession, and the sports events were the Football Association Cup Final, the Boat Race, a boxing match, tennis at Wimbledon, and an ice-skating competition. The third group,

[1] By eliminating the items about which the child cared very little, we hoped to make the choice a more meaningful one.
[2] For instance, close-ups of tennis at Wimbledon.

117

plays and entertainment, consisted of a play, an ice show, a musical concert, a panel game, a puppet show, and a ballet. Here the choice lay between being an audience at home and being taken out to a theatre or concert hall.

The fourth group, famous personalities, included a politician, an explorer, a film star, famous people in their homes, and the Royal Family. Interest in personalities is great and we wanted to see whether here the real contact would be preferred to the screen contact. The fifth group, the exhibitions and art galleries, were the Schoolboys' Own Exhibition, Windsor Castle, a museum and an art gallery. Except for the Schoolboys' Own Exhibition, these places do not greatly interest children of the two age groups with which we were dealing, and here we expected the convenience of television to win. In the final group (special places of work) were a fashion show, a motor-car factory, an airport, and Scotland Yard. Here, interest may be stimulated by television but not satisfied, so it was expected that the child would wish to see the real thing.

We calculated for each child six preference scores, one for each group. A child was given a positive score if he preferred to see on television more than half the items of a given group. Items in which he was not interested were excluded from this calculation.[1] Table 72 shows how much children prefer the real thing to seeing it on television.

TABLE 72. Percentage of viewers who would prefer to see more than half the items of each group on television rather than in real life

Class of items:	13–14 YEAR OLDS %	10–11 YEAR OLDS %
Ceremonial events	19	12
Sports events	20	22
Plays and entertainment	48	39
Famous personalities	10	4
Exhibitions and art galleries	23	18
Special places of work	19	19
Total cases (weighted)	516	516

In five out of the six groups some 80 per cent chose to see events and people for themselves. In the case of famous personalities the

[1] The method of scoring is relatively crude. Finer gradations were tried, but gave much the same result. They would, moreover, have been very cumbersome to calculate since each child had a different number of items in which he was interested.

118

percentages rose to over 90 per cent; only for plays, ballet, and concerts did the figure drop to 60 per cent. Where the choice is between watching entertainment in the theatre or concert hall and watching at home, the 'real thing' wins by only a narrow margin. But when it comes to going out to see processions, to visiting places, to seeing famous personalities, television is left far behind. Special mention must be made of sports events; here, too, the 'real thing' means sitting and watching a performance, but children's very strong interest in sport and hero worship of sports personalities lead them to prefer the actual event to the television version.

On the results of our findings, there is no difference between the intelligent and less intelligent, veteran and recent, or heavy and occasional viewers.

'*Viewing leads to "spectatorism" and loss of initiative.*' Those who make this criticism are advancing two related points: first, that the child will come to expect all his entertainment to be ready-made; and second, that this demand for the ready-made will eventually lead him to be less enterprising and resourceful generally. Our findings do not show that television induces a greater preference for ready-made entertainment, or that it renders viewers less active or less capable of showing initiative than controls.[1]

Previously we have shown that, where time has to be found for viewing, it is the other mass media, especially radio and the cinema, which suffer, and not playing with friends or taking part in some sport. Club attendance was hardly affected—with the possible exception of the cinema club.

Two open-ended questions about interests were asked: *There never seems to be enough time to do all the things one likes doing. Write down the three things you like doing best, that is in the time after school;* and: *Imagine you were spending an afternoon with a friend. What would you both be doing?*

The answers of viewers and controls were very similar; they both enjoyed the same sort of things—sport, playing, kicking a ball around, going for cycle rides, and so on.

We also devised an activity preference questionnaire entitled 'Which would you rather do?' Six different types of situation were presented, for each of which the child was offered the choice of taking part or watching. An example of a general question on sport was: *Which would you rather do: watch sport or games, or play in*

1 The Norwich study also showed that there was no difference in this respect between future viewers and controls.

sport or games? Specific sports such as swimming and skating, which are often shown on television, were similarly dealt with. In both, the active 'going swimming' or 'skating yourself' was contrasted with 'watching a swimming competition' or 'watching a skating contest'.

The other three situations were: learning to play a musical instrument (rather than 'listening to music'), making something (rather than 'buying it ready-made in a shop'), and finding one's way about with a friend (rather than being 'shown round a town by a grown-up who lives there').

TABLE 73. *Which would you rather do?*
Number of choices made in favour of doing things for oneself

(Maximum score = 6)

	13–14 YEAR OLDS		10–11 YEAR OLDS	
	V	C	V	C
Preference for doing things for oneself:	%	%	%	%
Low (below 4) . . .	20	23	17	18
Medium (4)	31	28	29	25
High (5 and 6) . . .	49	49	54	57
Total cases (weighted) . .	459	461	472	457

Table 73 shows once again that both viewers and controls preferred to do things for themselves. The one exception was learning to play a musical instrument—an activity which requires staying power, links up with schoolwork, and is, of course, related to a specific interest and ability. But here, too, viewers and controls behaved in much the same way.

Finally, we sought the co-operation of teachers, asking them to rate each child on the following three-point scale: *Shows a great deal of initiative, shows some initiative, lacks initiative.* Again, there was no difference between viewers and non-viewers.

'*Television leads to a jaded palate.*' The findings do not support this opinion; if anything, the reverse is true: viewers were more curious, more ready to interest themselves in a wide diversity of things—a difference which did not exist between future viewers and controls in Norwich. The livelier interest of viewers was shown in their responses to three different questionnaires. Children were presented with lists of different types of films and books, an inventory listing eighty different types of interests, and the 'preference for television versus real life' questionnaire which enabled them to say whether they were at all interested in seeing any of the items listed (Table 74).

TABLE 74. *How would you like to see them—in real life or on TV?*
Number of items out of 27 ticked as 'I am not interested in seeing this at all'

(Distribution of answers by age and intelligence)

13–14 YEAR OLDS

	All		Grammar		Sec. mod. I.Q. 100–114		I.Q. below 100	
	V %	C %	V %	C %	V %	C %	V %	C %
Not interested in:								
Less than 4 items .	37	36	35	39	31	35	42	34
4–9 items. . .	48	46	47	49	56	48	43	50
10 or more items .	15	18	18	12	13	17	15	26
Total cases (weighted) .	502	503	169	168	171	171	162	164

10–11 YEAR OLDS

	All		I.Q. 115 +		I.Q. 100–114		I.Q. below 100	
	V %	C %	V %	C %	V %	C %	V %	C %
Not interested in:								
Less than 4 items .	40	31	33	31	47	34	40	30
4–9 items. . .	45	41	56	44	37	39	40	42
10 or more items .	15	28	11	25	16	27	20	28
Total cases (weighted) .	505	502	170	166	170	171	165	165

Once again, we found that the influence of television depended on how receptive the child was and what alternative sources of stimulation were within his reach. Differences between viewers and controls were particularly significant among the dull adolescents and the bright 10–11 year olds. These children, despite their differing ages, were at much the same stage in intellectual development—a stage when the encouragement that television offers appears to fall on particularly fertile ground. It will be remembered that similar results were obtained when assessing the effects of television on values, attitudes, and knowledge.

'*Viewing dulls the imagination.*' This view is difficult to assess adequately by means of questionnaires, so we relied on information from the teacher. The children were rated on a three-point scale: 'Unusually imaginative; moderately imaginative; unimaginative.' Once again no differences were found between viewers and controls.

121

It is, however, likely that television influences the type of fantasy material produced much more than its quality or diversity. The younger viewers will now play at being the heroes of television Westerns or *Robin Hood*, just as those without television may identify with other types of Westerns and with heroes of books or radio plays.

It has been suggested that with both sound and vision provided, nothing is left to the imagination. But this argument would equally mean that radio plays and books are better stimulants for the imagination than the theatre, a point of view that is clearly untenable. It may be that some critics who use the argument are against television not because it occupies both eyes and ears, but because in their opinion much of what is presented is banal and stereotyped. The sophisticated adult may indeed find it so; but not the child, who is still trying to discover all he can about the rather bewildering world of adults and their relationships and problems.

There is, however, one small group of viewers—the television addicts—who showed signs of *spectatorism*, or lack of initiative and interest. But these children differed too much in other ways from the average viewer for their behaviour to be readily explained as an effect of television.

DOES TELEVISION ENCOURAGE CHILDREN TO BE MORE ENTERPRISING?

Our findings show that viewers were no more passive than controls; some viewers in fact seemed readier than the controls to be interested in a wide range of ideas and topics. Teachers often felt that children had become more receptive to new ideas.[1] Is it then possible to go further and claim that television encourages a child to take up new interests for himself?

Making things as a result of viewing

Over 70 per cent of the viewers had seen BBC competition programmes asking them to make models and drawings and to send them to the Television Centre.

We asked the children whether they had tried to make any of the things suggested, and also whether they had finished

---

[1] This was mentioned as one of the three most important effects by 21 per cent of the teachers.

anything and sent it to the Centre. The answers were as follows:

	13–14 YEAR OLDS	10–11 YEAR OLDS
	%	%
Finished something and sent off . . .	2	3
Finished something but not sent off . . .	6	10
Started something but not finished . . .	9	19
Had not tried to make any of the things shown .	83	68
Total cases (weighted)	387	399

It will be seen that only 3 per cent even of the 10–11 year olds had gone as far as finishing a model or drawing and sending it in. The figure for the older children was somewhat lower. Even in Norwich, in the first excitement of having television, the response was not greater; only 3 children out of 120 sent models to the Centre.

We allowed the children to interpret 'started to make something but not finished it' in the most lenient way possible; they were not restricted to any one programme, nor did we stipulate how much they need have done. Even then only 19 per cent of the younger and 10 per cent of the older children answered in the affirmative.

Neither intelligence nor social background distinguished those who attempted or completed models from the remainder of the viewers. The relevant factors seemed to be an interest in hobbies, in specific crafts such as woodwork and modelling, and also a general 'interestedness'.

Brian R., a 10 year old member of our group interview session, was a good example. He had sent a model in; and, characteristically, he had also responded to an invitation from another programme to send in old coins for identification. This is a boy with wide interests who responds to stimulation, from television as from other sources. The interviewer reports that he is well balanced and a highly intelligent child; television represents one item in a very full life.

Others sent models in because the topic offered on television fitted the children's established special interests.

One 10–11 year old boy had sent in a model aeroplane and also built a cutter. Asked what programme he could not get out of his mind, he mentioned a programme featuring model aircraft, and when asked what wish he would like Wilfred Pickles to grant, he said he would like to meet Neville Duke, the test-pilot.

Taking up new hobbies

Even among children of professional parents who encourage any sign of interest in a hobby, television appears to have very little effect. In their capacity as parents, ninety-four teachers were asked: *Has watching led your children to take up any new hobbies or interests or to give up any old ones?*

The ages of the children were from 2 to 16, and Table 75 below gives their replies separately, for two groups of children, the under-nines and over-nines. Apparently no hobbies were abandoned and very few were taken up as a result of viewing— apart from an increased interest in sport and athletics among the teen-agers (for which we have cited evidence throughout this report).

TABLE 75. Reports by teachers on hobbies or interests which their own children have taken up as a result of viewing

	UNDER 9 YEARS OLD	OVER 9 YEARS OLD
Hobbies or interests given up .	—	—
No new hobbies or interests developed	25	30
Hobbies taken up:		
Miscellaneous	5	2
Model making	1	4
Puppetry	2	—
Paper cutting, wire models .	2	1
Collecting things . . .	1	—
Sketching, painting . . .	2	2
Interests developed:		
Interest in wild life, bird-watching	2	—
Music and ballet . . .	1	—
Increased interest in sport . .	1	13
Total cases	42	52

(The figures represent actual cases, not percentages)

Visits to places of interest

An equally poor response was apparent from a study of a series of BBC children's programmes entitled *Treasure Hunt*: we carried out an inquiry into the frequency of visits to a museum following the display of its exhibits on this television programme.

Reading

Reading is the only activity which appears to have been encouraged by television. It has been shown that quite a number of children read books that have been dramatized on television. Here we were able to compare the relative effectiveness of radio for controls and television for viewers; among both younger and older children television emerged as the more potent stimulus.

CONCLUSIONS

Passivity. There is no evidence that viewing makes children passive. Using a variety of measures, we examined different ways in which such passivity might express itself. None showed a difference between viewers and controls. Viewers appeared to have as much initiative, imagination, and pleasure in active play as controls. Indeed, the activities they dropped to make room for viewing were in the main other forms of spectator entertainment: the radio and the cinema.

These findings differ from those of Belson on adults. He found that in some areas a restriction of interests took place during the first few years of viewing. Among children not even recent viewers responded in this way. Enjoyment in doing things is too integral a part of childhood to be readily ousted by television.

Stimulation. Many children read books that have been dramatized on television, and also gain a sense of interest in the subjects of non-fiction reading. But there were few signs of such interests translated into activities; nor did viewers go in more for hobbies, making things, entering for competitions, or visiting interesting places. Why, then, is television not more effective? Part of the difficulty lies in the nature of televised entertainment. The rapid succession of programmes makes it difficult for the child to stop and think about what he has just seen; his attention is at once diverted by the next programme. For this reason, television preaches mainly to the converted, to the child who has a strong interest and so needs little encouragement.

Serialized dramatizations of books may be more effective because each episode ends on a note of suspense. Psychological experiments on memory have shown that this technique, which avoids satisfying closure, and does not round events off, is an aid to retention and interest.

However, television has been successful in making adults *actively* interested in such unlikely subjects as archaeology. It would therefore be useful to know why viewing is not equally stimulating for children. Do programmes fail because the wrong topic is chosen, because they are poorly presented or because they require materials that are not readily available in the home? There is scope here for research to determine what activities are suitable and what are the most effective ways of getting them across. Such research should include details of exposition and display and determine what kind of person is particularly effective with the young viewers; how clear the instructions are, and how far the speed of giving instructions is suited to the age group for which the programme is intended.[1]

Until such studies are carried out, it would be premature to say that television is not a suitable medium for encouraging children to become more enterprising—all we can say is that at present its effects are negligible.

15   From: The Times, December 27th, 1969 Julian Critchley

Has television created a 'reality' of its own? As we spend nine years watching the box, it is as well to know how the medium can deceive. It holds up a mirror to society, but does the glass distort? We are bombarded by the prejudice of producer and performer, in a world where to assert is to prove, only the familiar faces of the pundit offer a kind of reassurance.

Television is the most powerful of media because we are asked to believe the evidence of our own eyes. We have to decide, when looking at news and current affairs programmes, not whether we should believe what we are told, but whether we can

[1] One of the authors of this report was asked by her 9 year old daughter to take down the questions at the end of a BBC children's programme on astronomy. Forewarned, with pencil and paper at the ready, and a university degree behind her, she was able to record three of five questions in full and one in part. One had to be omitted altogether. They were dictated at top speed, even though specialized terms were used.

st what we see. The camera may not lie—but what of the
aeraman? It is he who makes the camera's selection, and who
ates the terms, although the choice is made largely by the
of the screen itself, and it is someone else who provides the
mentary which tends often to amplify rather than to qualify
t we believe to be happening.
ne pictures choose themselves. The size of the screen, the need
to show action not inaction, and the necessity to compress the
events of 24 hours into minutes can together paint a picture of
'a barely recognizable world'.

Both in news and current affairs broadcasts the viewer is
swamped by information the effect of which has been not to
clarify but to confuse. In the words of David Holden, it has been
merely 'to turn up the decibels in the Tower of Babel'.

Television, perched as it is on the tip of a melting iceberg, is
both the most revealing and misleading of media. It has an
interest in disaster, it thrives best on conflict, crisis and controversy; all of which pass for what is called 'good television'. We
see the heaving of a brick, or the running on to the pitch; we do
not see the passivity and discipline of police (or demonstrators),
What we learn last of all, in the case of the Springboks, is the score.

Television has the power to change incidents into events, it
does not just exaggerate a story, as do newspapers; it can create
one. Its ability to produce self-generating news is plain; race
riots, student protests and the like have flourished in the rich
culture of publicity they have received.

What of balance? What can balance mean but arriving, even
instinctively, at one's own carefully balanced view? There can
be no such thing as a neutral, objective view of the facts, their
recognition is itself a partisan act. In current affairs in particular,
producers are more concerned to preserve what they see as their
editorial freedom.

There is, too, the facile categorization of countries into 'good'
and 'bad'. It cannot be denied that there is a community of
outlook between reporters and producers in current affairs. A
conformity of unconformity which is responsible for the predictability of so much television. The 'progressive' view, left-wing
in a trendy not ideological sense, is dominant. Its 'villains' would
include Enoch Powell, Quintin Hogg, and George Brown; its
'heroes' Nicholas Stacey, John Lennon, and Sir Ronald Gould.
The rise and fall of its idols can be traced all the way from a first
appearance on '24 Hours', through 'Late Night Line Up', to
the final indignities of 'Man Alive'.

To the inevitable prejudice is added the authority, albeit bogus, of the commentators. They are in manner flippant, judicial or commonsense plain, these *dei ex machina* to whom frequent exposure has lent prestige, and familiarity, omniscience. In this country, they are at least kept away from the news; they flourish late at night in magazine programmes. '24 Hours' recently carried an item on Vice-president Agnew's speech on the media. One after the other on film, American television pundits disapproved of what he had said. So did Mr David Dimbleby.

How ironical that one of the best of current television programmes should be called 'One Pair of Eyes', suggesting as it does the sheer novelty of personal prejudice. What effect does it all have? Television's tendency towards distortion is compounded by the power the medium extorts; for all too many 'telly' really is their 'window on the world'. Its stars are recognized as people we know—'Look there's David Frost'—for have they not been invited into our sitting rooms? Many have become witnesses to a world that is far more real than their own.

Some of us still cling to what is left of our convictions. For those with none, only inertia stands between them and the new 'reality'. The message of television is one of stimulation, agitation and change; what is less easy to see is its perpetual partiality.

16 From: New Society October 13th 1966

TELEVISION AND THE KENNEDY ASSASSINATION

Ruth Leeds Love
Bureau of Applied Social Research
Columbia University

The social contexts in which news organizations cover and report the news often intervene between a subject for news and the kind of coverage it receives. Thus the policies of a news medium owner, reinforced by his membership of various social groups, mean that his news organization will give heavy emphasis to some news subjects while virtually ignoring others. The characteristics of a reporter's contacts and his regular beat also lead to differential emphasis on and treatment of different news subjects. In addition, there are three other factors that help determine the kind of coverage a news subject is likely to receive. These are the newsman's *news judgments*, normative dimensions of *situational appropriateness* (in other words, the right mood or tone), and the exercise of *other party controls* (or outside influences and authority). To examine these factors I shall use incidents that arose during the networks' three and a half day continuous television coverage of President Kennedy's assassination.

The data to be used here come from 91 lengthy qualitative interviews conducted shortly after the assassination with personnel in the news division of ABC (American Broadcasting Company) and NBC (National Broadcasting Company), the news staffs of the networks' affiliate stations and several independent stations in Dallas, some Dallas newspaper editors and several wire service newsmen.

The news division broadcasters at all levels identify themselves as professional newsmen, many having worked previously in other news media. Like their newspaper counterparts, reporting is an ultimate value for them. They feel their job communicating news is important and gratifying, preferring it to other work. An NBC editor's comments are illustrative:

> *I am very proud to be in the business. I am happy to be a newsman, and I can't think of anything I would rather have been doing when (the assassination) happened. We had a part in history, and it is a little different from the people I know and live with. I think we all feel that way down deep inside. It was self-fulfilment, personally and professionally.*

A News Story

At the outset of the assassination period, which became known as the Black Weekend, news executives established the basic policy that the assassination would be covered like any other news story for it was a momentous and shocking event that raised many questions. As much news as possible would be broadcast in the time that became available through the cancellation of all commercial broadcasting.

Had the President died naturally commercial broadcasting would have been cancelled anyway for this action was premised on the normative consideration that cancellation is the only appropriate response to the death of the head of state, not on news

129

values. Had the President died naturally, however, there would have been no policy to cover the event like a news story. Whatever news there was about the President's death would have been reported and the long interludes between news would have been filled with appropriate memorial programmes, as was done when President Roosevelt died in 1945. As professional newsmen the broadcasters preferred covering Kennedy's assassination to Roosevelt's death. Some news executives explained:

> *It wasn't like Roosevelt's death . . . with Roosevelt everything went according to the book. Foreign nations sent the proper condolences; it was all done with the proper pomp and dignity. You knew what was going to happen. But it's different with the assassination. It's not all cut and dry. We were cops and robbers. Who did it? Was there a bomb?* (NBC executive.)

> *In FDR's case it was much harder. In Kennedy's case there was more news, the assassination, Oswald's death. With FDR it was a natural death, and the funeral train moving up from Warm Springs, stopping at each place, and covering Truman who was very reticent and then the funeral.* (NBC executive.)

The policy of staying with the story placed heavy demands on news material for it meant that only a minimum of nonhard news programming would be prepared to fill air time. In this way a producer would not find himself trapped in a discussion on the presidency when he wanted to switch to a news site. Virtually all available news was aired and what became available was largely determined by the articulation of the broadcasters' news judgments, their perceptions of what news was appropriate to the situation, and the exercise of other party controls.

Sacred and Profane

News judgment means determining what events are newsworthy and involves criteria of immediacy, relevancy and importance. The baselines for the criteria are perceptions of what affects the national interest and what interests the audience. During the Black Weekend news worth was determined largely by what was of immediate relevance to the assassination. Unrelated news events occurred at the time but they received scant attention, although on an ordinary weekend they would have been covered extensively. The broadcasters were totally involved with the assassination, both personally and professionally, so did not care to cover other news, claiming lack of audience interest in it. Moreover, they felt that switching from the sacred ceremonies

130

in Washington to other profane news would be in bad taste, disrupting the mourning mood. Only news that could affect American values as profoundly as did the assassination could be legitimately reported. An ABC producer explained:

> . . . the news editor came to me and said, (Aldous) 'Huxley died and there's a plane crash, do we want to do other news?' I said, 'We'll programme the death of the President.' I felt unless it was an outstanding piece of news we shouldn't do it. The problem was this—it's much more difficult to come from the scene in the Rotunda and have an announcer say, '. . . Huxley also died.' You can't equate the two. Now if Communist China had declared war on Russia we would have figured out a way to programme it but it would have had to be something that monumental.

News subjects or persons who control access to them exercise other party controls by saying yes or no to press requests for news and camera coverage. Because the broadcasters stress live television they may be more at the mercy of other parties than are other members of the press. If a news subject holds aloof from television cameras the broadcasters have little to show. The articulation between the broadcasters' newsgathering efforts and other party controls may determine whether a particular news story has led to the invasion of privacy or the infringement of civil rights or the abridgement of freedom of the press.

The third factor, perceptions of situational appropriateness, focuses on actions that can be interjected into a situation without disrupting its mood and tone. Following the assassination the broadcasters were most concerned about not airing material that might disrupt the national mood of sorrow and mourning, like news unrelated to the assassination. Several considerations of situational appropriateness guided the broadcasters in televising news.

One entailed concentrating on the culturally appropriate and expected responses of shock and horror to the assassination. The broadcasters added to the legitimacy of these responses by reporting mainly on appropriate reactions, both at home and abroad, to the assassination. Thus, on the day of Kennedy's funeral a cameraman did not film the people along the funeral route who were laughing en passant.

> I avoided taking shots of people laughing and smiling. I didn't think it was proper. There wasn't any bad behaviour but people do laugh.

Deviations from the appropriate responses, if televised, would detract from the mood the broadcasters wished to convey.

131

Like most newsmen, the broadcasters are on the alert for the unusual so they are not enthusiastic about covering expected, appropriate responses unless they are particularly apt, symbolizing the main news event. An NBC editor said:

> We went after the anti-Kennedy people . . . Welch . . . Wallace . . .
> Barnett and General Walker to get a balanced judgment but I wouldn't
> have cared if we didn't get . . . them, either professionally or personally
> . . . all they could say was, 'I'm sorry he is dead' or 'I am glad he is
> dead.' And it wasn't necessary to say the latter no matter how much
> anybody hated him.
>
> I would have done more man-in-the-street interviews . . . there were
> people huddling along the curb in blankets on . . . the day of the funeral
> in that biting cold. We did a few . . . and some of them were really
> beyond hoping for. They asked an eight year old boy why he came and
> he said, 'My mother and father didn't like Kennedy but he was our
> President and that's why I'm here.' Someone in New York called . . .
> to say that he summed it up better than anyone yet. (ABC executive.)

Standards of Taste

A second consideration focused on cultural standards of taste. News material that the broad middle class might deem offensive is consistently kept off the air, particularly if it is judged to have little news value. Correspondents refrained from describing President Kennedy's wounds and the fact that Mrs Kennedy was heard to say that she had her husband's brains on her hands.

A third consideration involved not marring the public images of public figures with incidental news reporting. If a person is popular, has a good public image, the broadcasters tend not to air material that contradicts the image, particularly in the context of live coverage of national events. An NBC producer said he would not have used the pictures immediately of Mrs Kennedy climbing onto the deck of the presidential limousine even if these had been available.

> I would have used (the pictures) considerably after the fact, not Friday
> . . . a sense of taste . . . it was a little too close to grief . . . Taste is a
> peculiar animal. I would have thought it was too soon to show it right
> afterwards . . . This is all hindsight on my part . . . Crawling out of
> the car was the kind of . . . you know, it left the wrong impression. I
> thought when I first saw it that not very great dignity was involved . . .
> (I don't think) she was fleeing . . . but that's the impression it left.

These three considerations all relate to the elusive concept of taste. To broadcast material that deviates from expected behaviour, does not accord with prevalent standards of taste and morality, or puts favoured persons in a bad light is to detract from the overall tastefulness and appropriateness of coverage. Such material would not only be offensive to public sentiment but to professional satisfaction, for the broadcasters pride themselves almost as much on producing a tasteful coverage as they do a comprehensive news coverage. An NBC executive said:

> *Technical flaws are quickly overcome. I assume that almost anything is possible technically. But more than most people, certainly more than the critics, I have a higher opinion not of the talents—that's assumed—but of the taste of the people in the business . . . the news departments of all the networkers are as tasteful as anything there is . . . In terms of taste, of course, it's what you leave out—assuming that anything is technically possible.*

Although the broadcasters cannot define what they mean by taste there is general but not universal agreement on what material can be broadcast. Another NBC producer indicated that he would have used the pictures of Mrs Kennedy even though members of the audience might have objected to the network.

> *About Mrs Kennedy, that wouldn't have bothered me. If we had used it we probably would have gotten calls but I wouldn't have hesitated because of that. I don't do things because of calls or no calls.*

How will Audiences Respond?

A fourth consideration bearing on situational appropriateness is how the audience will respond to broadcast material. Viewers can reward and sanction broadcasters by communicating with the networks, and some broadcasters take this into account. An ABC correspondent said that for trivial matters he considered potential audience sanctions.

> *I'm glad that there was no breach of taste . . . we were so exhausted and tempers were flaring . . . I was always afraid . . . that we might say something accidentally . . . another correspondent was very tired after 24 hours and then there were some pictures of Kennedy's furniture being moved out of his office. He began to say something like they might have waited at least until the President's body was cold. And then he collected himself at the last minute to say they might have waited until the President was buried . . . the idea of the President's body being cold might have been . . . bad taste and we would have gotten letters.*

The audience's capacity to sanction is a much less important control source, however, than its capacity to react emotionally and to be interested in what is broadcast. This form of control operates like an alter ego, reinforcing the broadcasters' commitment to professional norms and reminding them of norms and expectations held by the larger society. The audience *qua* alter ego is vague, for the broadcasters have no sharp image of the viewers, ascribing no specific social qualities to them. If they do ascribe characteristics they are their own so the broadcasters feel they can utilize their own concerns as guides to what concerns the audience.

At the same time the broadcasters feel they should not play on the audience's feelings by evoking responses in it beyond those already stimulated by the news itself. An NBC correspondent said:

> *Suddenly I found myself talking for (a few minutes) about John-John. I felt I had to. I recall saying that I will try not to get maudlin; I didn't want to arouse any sympathy in the audience by talking about a little child. I just had to talk about it; it may have been an emotional cathartic for myself.*

The desire not to arouse the audience's feeling derives partially from and reinforces the broadcasters' professionalism. In broadcasting a statement that might evoke audience feelings the broadcasters might also arouse their own feelings and portray emotion on the air which would be unprofessional. An NBC correspondent explained:

> *. . . everybody wanted to be careful, to be calm, not to permit emotion to show . . . It's just unprofessional . . . you don't have the right to impose your own feelings on any viewer . . . In . . . a tight situation you must keep a stiff upper lip . . . if you didn't panic might result . . . you must preserve a calm appearance, it's a matter of taste . . . and professionalism.*

The desire not to evoke feelings in the audience is also a control source operating independently of professional norms. One producer said that if the decision had been his he would not have permitted the interview with Officer Tippit's widow to go out.

> *I was damn mad they befouled themselves by interviewing Mrs Tippit, making her answer inane questions. The interview with her was an invasion of privacy, not only hers but mine too, it made my flesh crawl. Not (because of) what we were doing to her, but to the audience. The impact of television is much greater than of newspapers so things that*

were standard in newspaper days are much more repulsive on television, when you see them as moving pictures.

The broadcasters, then, attribute rights to the audience beyond the democratic right of being informed.

Dampening Fear

In addition, the broadcasters wish to dampen negative audience feelings like fear or panic. An NBC producer did not cover the story that SAC was alerted after the assassination for it might have contributed to potential panic in a time of crisis.

The broadcasters' efforts to dampen negative feelings in the audience was in part an effort to dampen their own fears. A correspondent who broadcast soon after news broke that shots were fired at Kennedy stressed that this was no time for speculation.

> *All I could do at this point was to offer caution. I guess I was reading a set of directions to our people as much as to the outside, let's not speculate . . . we will get the information to you as fast as we can . . . There is a great tendency to speculate when the President is shot, you can create pandemonium . . . I was concerned that this could have been a plot on the part of our adversaries . . .*

The projection of the broadcasters' own fears on to the audience was also apparent in their coverage of Lyndon Johnson. The day after the assassination a producer felt it was time to tell who he was and what he stood for.

> *This was very important because we were frightened . . . and we wanted to get this to the audience, dampen this fright in the audience. We didn't know (the audience was frightened) but there are not that many different types in the audience. We were frightened so we assumed they were, not the majority perhaps, but some of them . . . I believe the country is run by the President, all its crises are at least so we have to ask who is this man? I didn't mention on Friday that LBJ had a heart attack and that if he had another we'd get McCormick—then we'd all go to the storm cellars.*

An ABC correspondent said:

> *. . . I thought of how to ease the mind of the general public . . . We literally had the public in our power . . . An important part of our work was the coverage of Lyndon Johnson. Without exception the reports about (him) were highly favourable, but honest and it was the truth. We played up . . . his favourable qualities, Johnson as a man of strength,*

135

Johnson's ability to carry on. It needed to be said . . . at that time and it was said.

The broadcasters could go only so far in reassuring the audience about governmental continuity and Johnson's abilities. Too much emphasis would detract from mourning for Kennedy and give the impression that the nation might be better off with a new president. One correspondent believed that since Johnson knew Congress better than Kennedy he would succeed in having Kennedy's programme passed, yet this point could not be made easily without giving the wrong impression.

In sum, nothing should be broadcast which would violate the audience's expectations and definitions about a situation, or exacerbate the public's feelings about the news. The broadcasters' commitment to news norms, the reactions to broadcast material that they attribute to the audience and the possibility of audience sanctions combine to maintain the broadcasting of fare that is expected and appropriate to the situation.

Several incidents from the Black Weekend will illustrate how differences in articulation between news judgment, other party controls and the broadcasters' concern for situational appropriateness, affect coverage.

The coverage given to Oswald, from the moment of his capture on the Friday until the Sunday when Jack Ruby shot him, came about because the broadcasters judged him to be a crucial news figure, no normative considerations limited coverage, and other party controls, although expected, did not materialize. Since Oswald was the suspected assassin any news about him might help answer the central question of how and why the assassination happened. Network correspondents along with other newsmen waited long hours at the Dallas police station, hoping Oswald might pass by and talk, or that police officers might comment on the case.

A normative consideration that might have limited coverage was that extensive reporting would damage Oswald's right to fair trial. The correspondents in Dallas were mindful of this, one even telephoning the network about it.

I was a little concerned about the civil liberties question here so I called New York. But I got no satisfactory response. They said, 'You know we want to cover this big.' So I was in there pushing and shoving with everybody else.

News judgment, reinforced by network pressures, prevailed over the normative consideration. In practice, a suspect's right to due process of law has been weak and in this case, Oswald's right was further weakened by the broadcasters' felt obligation to reassure the audience through keeping it fully informed at a critical moment in national life. A studio correspondent who reminded the public about Oswald's rights, commented:

> *I wonder what sort of stories or speculation would have circulated if Oswald had been kept out of the news for 24 hours, what rumours about the police using third degree to get a confession, and the unusual protection afforded him. It would plant inarticulate fears in the people about what was done to him. The press had a responsibility to cover the story.*

The Media's Obligation
Given their professional interest and responsibility in covering news the broadcasters feel they cannot limit their own reporting efforts. A network field editor said:

> *It is the obligation of the news media to seek access to the news that is happening, and as close access as is possible. I don't think it is possible for us to limit ourselves to where we go. This is very possibly the responsibility of others in other fields—lawyers, doctors, policemen. But we must seek access to the news. Philosophically . . . in our system of checks and balances, freedom is never freedom when exercised by one party alone . . . We of the press cannot be the sole arbiter of what is freedom of the press.*

The Dallas police did not exercise the anticipated control for they felt obligated, in the public interest, to publicize their investigation of Oswald. They may not have realized that this could be done through pool coverage as well as through individual coverage by many news organizations. Police failure to control the press to any significant degree also arose from an incongruency between expectations governing Dallas press-police relations and expectations governing press-police relations in major cities like New York and Los Angeles.

The Dallas police seem to have little need to control the local press for Dallas newsmen know how far they may go in covering a police story: apparently that is much further than many other police departments allow. The latitude the police give the press in Oswald's case was not unusual. The Dallas police-press arrangement differs sharply from that of some cities where the press persists in news gathering until the police impose clear checks. A Dallas newspaper executive summarized the *impasse*:

> *The police in this case were subjected to types of newsmen they have never seen before . . . the very competent and aggressive newsmen who*

climb over people's backs to get pictures and a story. Here we work hard but we compete on a gentleman's level. There is no rough and tumble scrabbling of the type you get in New York and elsewhere. In New York you have seven or eight papers competing. This was a totally new element as far as the Dallas police were concerned.

Restraint over Mrs Kennedy

While Oswald's coverage came about through lack of articulation between news judgment, other party controls and normative considerations, the restrained coverage of Mrs Kennedy came about because there was articulation, albeit a vague one. Mrs Kennedy was covered whenever she appeared publicly and whenever the White House released information about her, for like Oswald she was a central news figure. Unlike news about Oswald, however, news about Mrs Kennedy did not serve the instrumental, affectively neutral function of informing the public, but provided an affective focal point for the news consumer, both because she was the President's widow and because she had established herself as a public figure in her own right. A news executive said:

It's natural that the widow is the central point in any story like this. There is the identification of people with her, especially the young people of the nation. This drew more attention to her than otherwise might be the case.

The restraint the broadcasters imposed on Mrs Kennedy's coverage derives partly from a bereaved person's right to privacy. Excessive coverage would have violated the right and indicated a departure from good taste. A news director said:

An effort was made to show Mrs Kennedy at various steps without leaving the camera on her too long in fear . . . of invasion of her privacy . . . Conscious effort was made . . . not to make any play on this lady's grief.

The restrained coverage was implemented partly through executive directive, partly through other party control, but primarily through the broadcasters' sensitivity to normative considerations. In keeping with the top news executives' general responsibility for maintaining tasteful newscasting an executive directed that for the funeral there should be no more intrusion on Mrs Kennedy than necessary. Other party controls consisted of a request from Mrs Kennedy's aides to the Washington network pool committee that cameramen refrain from taking head-on shots and close-ups of her and her children. Although executive directives and other party controls would have sufficed to insure tasteful coverage it is not clear that they were necessary or that they were even communicated to the broadcasters responsible for televising Mrs Kennedy. In several instances broadcasters subordinated news judgment to considerations of their own volition. An ABC producer said:

. . . I was struck throughout by the good taste that was spontaneously exhibited. There were no close-ups of Mrs Kennedy . . . (there was) no policy decision but individual cameramen showed restraint.

If the broadcasters had not limited themselves voluntarily it is quite likely that other party controls would have appeared quickly. A Washington news executive said:

(Andrew) Hatcher later said he heard no complaints (from the White House) about the coverage, that it was handled with great taste . . . (The Kennedys) had strong opinions about the coverage . . . you never got the feeling they would let you do anything to their disadvantage.

But not for Mrs Tippit

One wonders, then, to what degree the imminent probability of other party control contributed to self-limitation, and to what degree the broadcasters' awareness that the public might expect Mrs Kennedy's privacy to be respected reinforced their restraint. The questions arise for the broadcasters interviewed the widow of Officer Tippit who was slain by Oswald shortly after the assassination.

The broadcasters felt personally that an interview might invade Mrs Tippit's right to privacy but professionally they believed her story was news, and the only way it could be obtained was through contacting her for she lacked a public information apparatus. Here normative consideration was subordinated to news judgment. The broadcasters explained that if Mrs Tippit felt her privacy threatened she could have declined to speak with reporters. Thus a problem for normative considerations was defined to be a problem for other party controls. A film editor said of the Tippit interview:

We went after Mrs Tippit in Dallas . . . there was a question of trading on her emotions but . . . there was a need for a follow-up on (the policeman's death) and I did ask for the (interview). I ask for things I don't agree with when we are covering a story . . . Mrs Tippit was willing but we wouldn't have forced the issue.

A Dallas correspondent explained:

> *I had to interview Tippit's widow . . . I thought . . . it was an invasion of her privacy. I am still a little shaky about interviewing somebody right after a death . . . the interview went well and she was cooperative . . . I suppose it helped the family in the fund drive . . . I think the desk in New York was right in making the assignment. It had to be told.*

The different coverages given to the widows might be explained by their different abilities to exercise other party controls, and to reinforce normative considerations, based on their different statuses. Mrs Tippit was an ordinary citizen until her husband's murder cast her into the limelight so she would have had no experience with the press and might not have known how to exercise her technical right to say no had she wanted to do so. There was little likelihood that Mrs Tippit would limit the press. In contrast, Mrs Kennedy as the First Lady had considerable experience with the press and knew how to protect her privacy. It is unlikely that any newsman would have been permitted to interview her. Mrs Kennedy's high status may also have reinforced the broadcasters' commitment to good taste, if for no other reason than awareness that the public would expect it.

No Party Politics

The broadcasters declared a moratorium on party politics, believing that investigation of how Kennedy's death would affect the 1964 presidential election was irrelevant to the main story and a matter that could be handled 'even after the funeral' to quote one news executive. The decision not to cover politics involved both news judgments and normative considerations.

Political news at this time would have been in bad taste. Kennedy was assassinated in his capacity as the symbolic and actual leader of his country, not as the leader of the Democratic party. Johnson was perceived to be the new head of state, not the new Democratic President. Partisan politics, then, were not germane and their examination would contaminate the sacred mourning period with a graceless secular element. Consistent with this nonpartisan view of the assassination, the broadcasters always had Congressional leaders of both parties on television to discuss the country's political institutions.

Even if taste had not eliminated politics the broadcasters would have been hard pressed for news. No partisan political events were happening to provide news nor could any be generated through interviews. Politicians were expected to exercise other

SUMMARY CHART OF ARTICULATION AND EFFECTS OF THREE FACTORS

news subject	news values	situational appropriateness	other party controls	outcome
Lee Harvey Oswald suspected assassin	intensive coverage favoured because it would answer important questions about assassination	recognition of suspect's right to fair trial weak/ audience perceived as having to be informed	very few/suspect powerless to exercise controls/police controls expected but police unaccustomed to checking newsmen	intensive coverage that interfered with police work and presented difficulties for fair trial
Mrs Kennedy, the president's widow	coverage favoured because she was affective news figure with whom public identified	right to privacy strong because of high status and public image/public would be offended by coverage that violated privacy	a few requests to limit coverage/high probability of controls if inappropriate material broadcast. Mrs Kennedy accessible only through 'gatekeepers'	restrained, tasteful coverage that received compliments from critics
Mrs Tippit, widow of police officer slain by Oswald	coverage favoured because of her connection to events	right to privacy weak because of ordinary status/public unlikely to be concerned about her privacy	none/low probability for any because she had no experience with press	interview conducted and broadcast/some broadcasters object/ some complaints from viewers to networks
partisan politics	coverage not favoured because no news at time. Too early to assess political effects of assassination	secular politics in very bad taste during sacred mourning period	political figures refused to make political statements at time	brief mention of partisan politics after funeral

141

party controls, if for no other reason than the knowledge that political statements at this time might boomerang in the future. One broadcaster said, 'You couldn't have gotten anyone to say anything political.' Both networks reported incidents where a reporter did address a political question to a political figure and was promptly squelched. A producer said:

> *I remember throwing out an interview with Goldwater done not by one of our men but by a reporter with an affiliate station who asked how this event affected the 1964 political campaign. Goldwater blew up, and I thought that using (the interview) would (only) compound the bad taste . . . Goldwater was obviously right, the reporter in bad taste.*

The coverage of Oswald, Mrs Kennedy, Mrs Tippit and partisan politics only illustrates how news judgment, other party controls and normative considerations articulate with each other to help determine the coverage news subjects receive. Comparison of these incidents suggests that neither normative considerations alone nor the probability of other party controls alone is sufficient for the broadcasters to initiate limits on coverage when news judgment justifies its pursuit. Combined, however, the two factors seemingly limit news coverage, at least when a subject is not judged overly crucial for keeping the public informed. Whether the broadcasters would limit or pursue coverage until other parties check them when news judgment strongly warrants it, but both normative considerations and the probability of other party controls weigh against it, is an open question. The matter is worth further study, however, for the net result of the articulation of the three factors seems to be a coverage that heightens whatever social solidarity and reaffirmation of values a news event itself evokes in the poulace. While this effect may be desirable when collective events like the inaugurations are covered, so substantiating McLuhan's idea that television retribalizes society, it is questionable when other events are covered.

SECTION III The Film

The film has social and aesthetic implications. It clearly does not, in the Western world, possess the quantitative significance as a medium that it did two or three decades ago. Nowadays people tend to go to see a film, and not to the cinema. Still, the weekly admissions rate to the cinema in Britain is the equivalent of about 15 per cent of the population. Many more people watch films—not all of them ancient—on TV. And as an art form, the film has had an exceptionally rich decade. On both major counts, the film is among the largest and most interesting areas of the communications industry.

Of the many varieties of film the audiences watch, perhaps two deserve special mention. The 'blockbuster' is hardly, as Hall and Whannel suggest, a 'risky gamble'; it is, on the contrary, a near-certain success. Its formula is universality, and it thus embodies one of the forces which have been discerned in public broadcasting. The other is the experimental, high-art film. Such films have had surprisingly wide acceptance of recent years; there is no question of the capacity of Antonioni, Fellini, Truffaut, and so on to reach a wide if not mass audience. But such films reflect the director's concern to develop his own language of communication. If, then, one looks at the film

143

industry as a whole, one might incline to accept Hall and Whannel's view that the film is 'a bridgehead of communication between cultures or classes'. But if one looks at the experimental area of the industry, one sees a passionate concern with the nature and techniques of communication, that accepts the idea of a more limited audience.

Some useful questions are posed by Michael Roemer. He points out that the film operates through conventions. 'Convention' is 'a coming together', an implicit agreement between director and audience on the terms of communication. It is absolutely necessary. Yet, as Roemer points out, many conventions after the passage of years appear banal, wooden, predictable. Which conventions are permanent; which require revision? Should revision be a process of evolution or radical break? Again, Roemer reminds us of the basic problem inherent in the use of the camera. Does it point with a kind of neutral authority towards an 'objective' reality? Or does it reveal, subjectively, the images that press upon a beholder? 'Subjective' and 'objective' shots may succeed each other in the same film, but they both point towards the ambiguous status of the camera. Penelope Houston tells us something of the major concerns of directors in the most recent past. Conventions have been very drastically defied. But does this merely substitute a new set of conventions for the old? The capacity of directors to feed upon, quote from, allude to, or simply plagiarize films of the recent past is remarkable. For instance, the hand-held camera, the blurred image, the apparently disconnected cut have become clichés. In search of the spontaneous, the directors must run a paradoxical risk of imprisonment in a modish trap.

The basic issue of communication, posed by the latest films, is this. Our leading directors seek to develop a new and personal language of communication. The work of the best of them has undoubtedly become meaningful to a wide audience. But to communicate, signs are required. We may call them conventions; the words used here are conventional. New signs, new conventions are constantly being created. The question therefore is whether the accelerated growth of new conventions can, on the one hand, satisfy the foremost directors that an adequate language for their discourse exists; and on the other hand, can maintain contact with a mass audience largely used to much older conventions. It seems likely that the general process of media transference, and particularly the reciprocal relationship between film, TV-drama, TV-documentary, and the films shown on TV, have speeded up considerably public assimilation of new conventions.

And finally: this area of communications reveals, perhaps, most clearly the situation of the whole. The great media are organized as separate realms, but in reality compose an entity that is in a constant state of fermentation, or of inter-pollination. The core of the situation, for many of the communicators, is the creative tension between the necessity for convention, and the necessity for innovation and experiment. But the field of communications as a whole advances one central problem that dominates all the others: the still-unanswered questions of the long-term (rather than the immediate) effects of the communications revolution upon the mass public.

17 From: The Popular Arts, Stuart Hall and Paddy Whannel

Like jazz, the cinema is an available popular form. Although attendances have declined sharply, the current rate of approximately 8 million admissions per week shows that the cinema habit is still a strong one. It is possible to 'drop in' to the movies in a way that one cannot to the theatre—even where there is a theatre to go to. And the public for the movies is predominantly a young one.

The capacity of the film as a vehicle for the self-expression of the artist—popular or otherwise—is less apparent than in jazz. The complicated technical procedures of making films, the dependence on a large team of craftsmen and technicians, the pressures of heavy investment, all combine to make it difficult for film-makers to impress their personalities on their work. What is indeed remarkable is the number of those who *have* been able to evolve a personal style. Even more relevant for us is the achievement of the cinema as a popular art. In the early days, the cinema drew heavily on popular drama, stage spectacles and the music-hall comedy. The early films in Britain were often first shown in the halls, and the audiences for those earlier forms became the audience for the cinema. Indeed, long before critics spoke about Chaplin and D. W. Griffiths, the work of these artists was immensely popular. The early film comedies, in the way they defended the underdog, burlesqued authority and inflicted indignity on the rich and pompous, reveal something of the way the cinema reflected popular tastes and attitudes. So did the unabashed sentiment, the pathos and the full-blown romance of the 'melodramas of the heart'.

This popular quality of the cinema as an institution is now threatened from both ends. As the cinema begins to move towards high art, it caters more naturally for the educated, middle-class audience familiar with the more traditional forms. This development is good, in so far as it brings the cinema in touch with the standards of high art, and makes it a medium of complex and subtle communications: but it can help to stratify the audience, and affect adversely the quality of its more popular work. At the other end is the growth of the 'blockbuster' film or spectacular. Those endlessly long, tedious and over-blown productions—a risky gamble by the film studios to hold on to a declining audience—with their printed programmes, booked seats, non-continuous showings, are 'films for the people who don't go to the pictures'. If *L'Année Dernière à Marienbad* and *Vivre sa Vie* represent the evolution of a popular art towards high art, *Ten Commandments*, *Around the World in 80 Days*, *King of Kings* and *South Pacific* mark the decline of a popular art into mass art. Bearing in mind the general distinction which we tried to draw earlier between popular art and mass culture, consider the remarks of Penelope Houston on the 'blockbuster':

If the blockbuster banks on its difference from other films, however, it must at the same time assume universality. It must break through *all* the audience barriers, so that it can be sure of an all-class, all-income, all-nationality public. To this end, it must be carefully and deliberately disinfected, as a matter of production policy, of any attitudes which might annoy anyone, anywhere. War films must be neutralized (like *The Longest Day*); religious films must keep in mind religious minorities (like *King of Kings*), though they can afford the luxury of rebuking Imperial Rome; producers, remembering that half their prospective audience is outside America, must be wary of any theme which bears so directly on the American scene that it lacks appeal for foreigners. Westerns, of course, are exempt: Hollywood long ago converted the western into international currency.

The word *must*, in this context, really is a categorical imperative: once the investment has been made, and the initial risk taken, the film is committed to certain box-office demands.

Sight and Sound, Spring 1963

Nevertheless, a number of popular cinema forms—such as the western, the thriller and the musical—have developed; and although most examples of these genres are banal, routine treatments of well-worn formulae (as is common in mass art), a number of gifted popular artists have been able to fulfil themselves while working within this popular tradition and using the familiar conventions. Even the spectacular can, at times, be made to work in this way. This line of work, which we mark off as distinct from either high art or mass art in the cinema, is a continuing thread of creative achievement in a mass medium. It is also a thread which links together a good deal of the work which we discuss favourably in this study. And where more debased work is critically examined, popular art represents a kind of touch-stone of quality which informs our criticism.

A final point should be made about the cinema in particular. There is a quality about the medium of film which makes it peculiarly accessible as a popular art. It is, as John Grierson said, a *physical* medium. The experience of watching a film makes a direct impact on us—the 'darkened auditorium, the dominating screen, with its very large, moving figures, its very loud sound, its simultaneous appeal to eye and ear' (Williams, *Preface to Film*). This has its dangers—allowing 'inferior artists to gain apparent effects by a process of powerful suggestion rather than of artistic expression'. But it also has compensating advantages: the film, which we feel so directly and immediately, can often by-pass some of the social and cultural barriers that cut off audiences from material in the more traditional arts. Modern media like the cinema, though so frequently misused, do have this potential for undermining the established hierarchies of culture, simply because they hold an effective bridgehead of communication between cultures or classes, and access to them cannot be tightly controlled. We have yet to see what would happen if these

147

channels of communication were really cleared for work of quality: the cultural leap could be enormous. It would be foolish to exaggerate. The best cinema—like most advanced jazz—seems to push towards high art: average films or pop music are processed mass art. But this only makes the really popular work in both forms the more significant.

18   From: The Contemporary Cinema by Penelope Houston

Towards a New Cinema

New cinema, new wave, new American cinema, Italian renaissance: the phrases crop up, forming a convenient kind of critical shorthand, which like most shorthand can be effectively read back only by the writer. Of course nothing is really new, so that antecedents can always be traced, ancestors run to earth; and of course new waves all too soon begin to look like tired conventions. One thing, however, seems certain. In the doldrums of the middle fifties, it would have been difficult to write a survey of this kind without casting sneaking glances over one's shoulder towards the supposed golden ages of film-making. Neorealism was dying with the whimper of an *Il Tetto*, British cinema somnolent, the French industry given over to a professionalism that masked an absence of original thought, Hollywood still narcissistically enchanted by the size of its own screens. Lethargy seemed to be creeping up, as though the cinema felt television closing up on it and had half-hearted ideas of conceding the race. Now, looking back, the period around 1956 seems a watershed: between the neorealists and the *nouvelle vague*, or (and this is not simply another way of saying the same thing) between a middle-aged cinema and a young one.

It was certainly time some of the rules were broken, technically as well as aesthetically. Raoul Coutard, the brilliant French cameraman, shoots straight into the light in *Lola*; the ubiquitous hand-held camera gets close in among the crowds; *Hiroshima mon*

148

Amour obliterates the flash-back; Antonioni takes over a golf club to shoot part of *La Notte*; Woodfall rents a house for *A Taste of Honey*; everyone, everywhere, discovers the advantage of making films outside studios, so avoiding that systematization which manages to impose the same kind of technical stamp on each and every subject. What the cinema of the middle fifties needed, to shake it up, was some artists prepared to have a go, to smash up a few conventions just to see what the pieces looked like. The fact that it found them, in France, spurred on other people. Everyone wanted a *nouvelle vague*, even if the French decided, as soon as they had it, that they were not entirely sure what they had got hold of. As a result, and to an extent unthinkable only a few years ago, we are living in the age of the first film. Godard, Truffaut, Varda, Demy, Pasolini, Olmi, Patroni Griffi, Polanski, Reisz, Schlesinger, Cassavetes: none of these have had to serve an apprenticeship in B-features, to await the moment of critical recognition. Festival entries tend to be divided between the films of the cinema's great and now ageing artists (Renoir, Bunuel, Ozu), of its post-war generation (Antonioni, Wajda, Torre Nilsson, Bergman) and of its established and unestablished newcomers. Missing on the whole, is the generation from the first decade of sound.

As always, the reaction is against the recent past. But although there is something just tangible enough to be called a new way of looking at the cinema, there certainly is no such thing as a collective spirit. Any generalization based on one group of films can be smartly cancelled out on the evidence of another. If there is no common ground between, say, Godard and Antonioni, there is not much more between Godard and Resnais, his fellow-countryman. But *some* movies, it can be said, are more spontaneous than they used to be, more inclined to snatch at the fleeting moment; they relish ambiguity, the kind of Pirandellian situations in which characters are always going in search of their own identities, are not even entirely sure where life ends and film begins: they are based on a knowledge of the cinema's past which enables them to use quotation and allusion, to work within a frame of reference necessary to the creators if sometimes perplexing to the audience; they look as though the people making them enjoyed what they were doing; and they admit their own imperfections.

Should one [to quote Truffaut] continue to pretend to be telling a story which is controlled and authoritative, weighted with the

149

same meaning and interest for the film-maker and for the spectator? Or ought one rather to admit that one is throwing on the market a kind of rough draft of one's ideal film, hoping that it will help one advance in the practice of this terribly difficult art?

Any number of young artists are engaged in this exploration; and are assuming, as directors have not been able to do on this scale since the twenties, that they have a right of discovery, that the whole industrial framework of studios and big companies ought not to stand in their way. In America, inevitably, the problem comes most clearly into focus. From a round-table discussion published in the California magazine *Film Quarterly*, one extracts two quotations. According to the producer John Houseman:

> Think how very few American films, even among the good ones, have a signature. This has something to do with the organization of the studios and the releasing companies, but it also has a lot to do with the audience. There is a very strong resistance to individual statements in American pictures, while among the worst European film-makers there is nearly always some kind of personal statement.

From Irvin Kershner, one of the younger American directors:

> How do you make a film which is entertaining, which has ideas, which is let's say adult, which doesn't depend on violence for its shock, doesn't depend on sex for its excitement—how do you create this kind of drama for $200,000 when there's no time to play, to waste, to take a chance to do all the things that an artist has to do to make a film?

The director is talking practically, in terms of the low-budget film made within the industrial system, and the producer theoretically. But both are preoccupied with this question of a 'signature,' of the stamp of personality as something which ought to be burnt into a film. A few years ago, in a Hollywood more easily confident of its own considerable assets, the distinction between one kind of movie and another might have been taken for granted, or at least accepted as a fact of cinema life. Now it has to be argued out, with the implication, which by no means all Europeans would subscribe to, that Europe, has got the upper hand.

An answer, of a sort, is to work outside the studios; and within the last few years there has been a good deal of talk about a new

American cinema, New York based, independent, radically minded. Some critics have resolutely battled to extract evidence of a 'movement' from films made in half a dozen styles: from Lionel Rogosin's dramatized documentary of Skid Row, *On the Bowery*, to John Cassavetes's improvised actors' exercise, *Shadows*; from Shirley Clarke's *The Connection*, which wraps its study of junkies waiting for a fix within the elaborate protective cocoon of a film within a film, to Richard Leacock's television documentaries, where a remorseless camera moves close in on a football match or an election meeting; from the short-film work of numerous avant-garde experimentalists to the low-budget features with a toe-hold in the commercial market.

Jonas Mekas, a New York critic and one of the most energetic propagandists for this whole elusive idea of a new American cinema, sees it as

an ethical movement, a human act . . . It was in his quest for inner freedom that the new artist came to improvisation. The young American film-maker, like the young painter, musician, actor, resists his society . . . He cannot arrive at any true creation by reworking and rehashing ideas, images and feelings that are dead and inflated—he has to descend much deeper below all that clutter. His spontaneity, his anarchy, even his passivity, are his acts of freedom. [Further, argues Mekas] . . . If we study the modern film poetry, we find that even the mistakes, the out-of-focus shots, the shaky shots, the unsure steps, the hesitant movements, the over-exposed, the under-exposed bits, have become part of the new cinema vocabulary, *being part of the psychological and visual reality of modern man* [my italics].

Part of the vocabulary these things are, though in employing resounding theory in defence of practical inadequacy, Jonas Mekas hardly makes the out-of-focus shots seem any less blurred. A shaky camera is much more likely to be evidence of financial stringency or practical inexperience than of sincerity. But it becomes very easy to get into a state of mind in which roughness is equated with honesty, in which the more raw and unfinished and obviously unprofessional a film looks, the more fervently it will be held to be asserting its independence. (Then, unfairly, Hollywood strikes back by trying to give some of its movies the fashionable grainy look of hard actuality.)

Resistance to Hollywood's pluperfect technique, precisely because it is Hollywood, and professional, and expensive, goes with

151

the kind of unfocused protest against society and its works which turns a film such as Mekas's own *Guns of the Trees* into a tirade of outrage. Here the Americans part company with the markedly unpolitical French. But they come together again in their feelings about improvisation, the value of the film which evolves its own sense of direction as it goes along. In itself, improvisation can hold a different meaning for almost any film-maker who experiments with it. Jean Rouch, in a film such as *Chronique d'un Été*, uses the camera as a kind of psychiatric tool, allowing it to form a third in conversations in the belief that in its admonitory presence people are closer to revealing the truth about themselves. But he also shoots hours of footage, and it is in the editing of this that the film emerges. Truffaut and Godard improvise when it suits them. John Cassavetes, in *Shadows*, made a film which announced itself proudly as a work of total improvisation, in which the validity of any given moment depended on the degree of response the actor managed to bring to it. Improvisation may achieve that spontaneity many film-makers long for. But few directors, after all, arrive at their results through a single take, and what was spontaneous at the beginning of the day's shooting may by the end of it have become something quite different.

Advocates of improvisation, though, are much more concerned with the idea of release: the freeing of the actor to make contributions going beyond the range of his part, as the script records it, the freeing of the camera from any rigidly preconceived plan: the freedom, in fact, to invent at the moment of shooting, to send the film off at a tangent if it seems a good idea. Many of these semi-improvised films inevitably look embarrassingly naïve: a bad actor speaking good lines is probably a happier sight than a bad actor struggling to communicate some ill-defined, ineffable inner something or other. Even when the improvised film works, as *Shadows* mostly did, it seems to do so as a once-for-all experiment, a stage in a director's career which he could not revisit if he tried, and where others follow him at their own risk. The film-maker probably has to go through technique to emerge safely on the other side, needs to know exactly what effect he's after before he sets other people loose to achieve it for him. Directors of greater *naïveté* are liable to waste as much footage on pursuing their players aimlessly around, waiting for the elusive and significant truth to hit them like a thunderbolt, as Hollywood does on tracking its stars through romantic locations. And, of course, the conventions pile up: the dead-into-camera monologues, the shots of rubbish heaps,

152

stretches of wasteland, all the well-worn symbols of city squalor which creep like so much ivy over experimental films.

Essentially, these improvised and semi-improvised works see their function not as a controlling and shaping of experience, the discovery of a pattern or logic in a series of events, but as a baring of immediate emotion, and the shattering of expected patterns through the intervention of the haphazard and the unplanned. Art itself is a word such film-makers might not care to accept too readily, because of its connotations of tradition and discipline. A moment of direct emotional truth can bite deep beneath the surface. *Shadows* pulls off such a moment, for instance, in the needling dialogue between the white boy who has come to take the coloured girl out for the evening, the girl resentful of his colour and her own, and her two brothers. And although such piercing insights may be few and far between, and the film-maker may not always be able to regulate their coming, or to sort out the absolutely genuine from the just-off-the-mark, they are the justification of his method. Film-making, like bird-watching, creeps up on the truth.

Improvisation is a technique and a tool, and one which many contemporary film-makers reject. It is an interesting exercise to compare the published texts of such films as *L'Année dernière à Marienbad* or *L'Avventura* with the pictures themselves, to see the extent to which two films very precise in their structure had a prior existence on paper, and also to note the points at which the director has moved away from the original text. Film-making is not an exact science: areas for improvisation always remain open. The creative process is continuous, from the thinking that goes on before the film actually goes into production, to the changes in the original conception effected at the shooting stage, to the final shaping of the picture during the editing.

'I go away by myself for half an hour or so before we begin shooting,' says Antonioni, and 'you might say I was inventing a little bit of film.'

'I arrive in the morning knowing what I intend to do during the day, but not how I intend to do it,' says Bresson.

'I have an idea at the back of my mind, and I develop it with my actors; although we work from a written text, the dialogue may be put down on paper only a few minutes before we start filming,' says Godard.

Use of actual locations, for interior as well as exterior scenes, has also cut down on some of the elaborate pre-planning customary where sets have to be constructed to order in the studio.

Another pointer for the new cinema, and one which links directors who otherwise have little in common, is the kind of relationship the film-maker assumes with his audience. Increasingly, he tells them as much as he cares to, and they take it from there. When one talks of the film as moving closer to the novel, this is to some extent what one means: that it addresses itself to each of us as an individual, that it deals in ambiguities of motivation and relationship which it is for us to elucidate, that it assumes our familiarity with the grammar of the screen. What does it mean? It means what you think it means. 'Am I to sympathize with this character or not?'—'I've shown him to you as I see him, now it's for you to make up your mind.' This is the sort of dialogue set up between spectator and director. Why does Anna disappear in *L'Avventura*, and what has happened to her? Have the man and the woman in *L'Année dernière* met last year, or this year, or never? Why does Patricia betray Michael in *A Bout de Souffle*, and what are we to make of her last enigmatic close-up? Why does Jeanne Moreau drive her car off the broken bridge in *Jules et Jim*? Are the various women we encounter in *Lola* meant to express aspects of Lola herself—Lola as she was as she will be, as she might have been? Audiences may ask the questions, and critics speculate, at enormous length, about the answers. The directors concerned know that they have made the questions irrelevant, or have answered them to their own satisfaction.

It would not do to make too much of this: the cinema is in no danger of becoming as esoteric as all that. But it is, on a previously unprecedented scale, testing out some of its own powers, its ability to move freely in time as well as space, its ability to withhold as well as to deliver information, to surprise, and confuse. In Roger Leenhardt's *Rendezvous de Minuit* there is a café episode in which the conversation turns on the possibility that one of the new film-makers, from the shelter of a newspaper kiosk, is at that moment turning a hidden camera on the scene. A joke; a critic's conceit (Leenhardt is critic as well as film-maker); an affectation; and also a comment by the cinema on the cinema, on its determination that we should take it on its own terms, remember that we are sitting in a theatre watching a film, and adjust our conception of reality to admit that in the present-tense grammar of the movies there is only the reality of what is *now* on the screen.

Whether all this should be regarded as merely fashionable, or as symptomatic of the way art reacts to a disordered and confused

154

society, a world in which areas of certainty contract, and judgements become relative, it certainly relates to another trend in contemporary film-making. A reaction has set in against the cinema of straightfoward social purpose, and a *Grapes of Wrath* or a *Bicycle Thieves*, a *Stars Look Down* or a *Terra Trema*, is not very likely to be made today by any of the major film-makers in the West. Underlying many of the really significant films of the last few years is an unspoken sense that the public context, the social scene in all its complexity, is something too big to grasp and too unwieldy to be susceptible to change. We have a cinema of personal relationships, private worlds, with anti-heroes engaged in splicing together the broken and rough ends of personality, or in pursuing illusions half-recognized as such; an amoral cinema, or one endeavouring to construct its morality through a series of *ad hoc* judgements. *Hiroshima mon Amour* is not about peace or the Bomb, as much as it is about a woman trying to live with her past. *Shadows* is not about the colour question, as much as it is about a coloured family whose attitudes to each other are at least as relevant as their feelings about the way the world treats them; *A Bout de Souffle* is not about crime, but about Jean-Paul Belmondo and Jean Seberg; *La Notte* is not a tract on modern marriage. Within their context, these films are not uncommitted or disengaged works, but their commitments remain essentially to individuals. Any generalizations we care to make really become our own affair; and the films accept no responsibility (as did *The Grapes of Wrath* or *Bicycle Thieves*) to offer them on our behalf.

In an essay on the novel, Mary McCarthy has complained that what modern fiction lacks is the factual context: the calm, detailed, *interested* description of how factories are run, how a town is put together as a social organism, the accumulation of facts about freemasonry or whaling or the Chancery Courts, which characterized the nineteenth-century novel. Elsewhere she has written:

> The writer must be first of all a listener and observer, who can pay attention to reality, like an obedient pupil, and who is willing, always, to be surprised by the messages reality is sending through to him. And if he gets the messages correctly he will not have to go back and put in the symbols, he will find that the symbols are there, staring at him significantly from the commonplace.

Such comments could be applied with almost equal relevance (which is hardly surprising) to the contemporary cinema. The artist's passion for putting in the symbols, like so many currants in a cake, and the critic's for pulling them out again, rapidly enough become a bore. And the film, as well as the novel, seems to be moving away from the period when information, the assembly of facts, engaged its major artists. If the cinema robbed the novel of much of its journalism and factual reporting, television has done the same thing to the cinema.

A cinema preoccupied with personal relationships and subjective landscapes may find itself losing contact with this hard, limiting, disciplinary, and necessary world of fact. But the cinema is also a more objective medium than the novel, in the most simple sense of the novelist being able to move so exclusively into areas of subjectivity that he no longer feels any need to tell us what his people and places look like, while the film must always, and by its nature, surround its characters with the clutter of their material existence. Even if we see events through the eyes of a central character, we also remain outside him, evaluating his actions as we watch them on the screen. Even a *L'Année dernière*, with its open invitation to a subjective response, is filmed objectively. The novelist may describe a scene, and forget it: the movie can hardly get away from its own scenery.

Insomuch as there is a new cinema worth talking about, it is because a number of directors are very consciously thinking in terms of how screen language can be made to work for them. They are more interested in the way things look and feel and sound than in what they signify in general terms; more interested in mood than in narrative; more concerned with how people behave and give themselves away in action than with how they might choose to see themselves. They are asking from their actors not the great neon-blazing star turns but performances which break through the hard professional surface: at the worst, an emotional strip-tease; at the best, a revelation. In players such as Jeanne Moreau and Monica Vitti, Jean-Paul Belmondo and Marcello Mastroianni, they have acquired willing accomplices. Above all, they give us the sense of the film itself as a risky and unique creative adventure.

Any amount of nonsense has been produced during the last few years by directors whose main creative activity consists in taking over other people's mannerisms. Entertainment-film clichés may afford restful and tranquillizing evidence that the conventions are still in working order. New-wave clichés are deadly because they come from directors trying to pass them off as new currency. But all this was to be expected. The cinema moves a few steps closer to the minority arts: its passion for allusion and quotation, for instance, is not really very far distant from the point reached by poetry almost forty years ago; and its emphasis on the immediate can not too implausibly be related to action painting. And as it moves, so it acquires the affectations along with the advantages. Antonioni occupies the painter's traditional position: far enough back from his subject to give us our sense of dramatic distance. Some of the young French directors keep our noses pressed up against it; we can distinguish a brilliant blob of colour here, some dashing brushwork there, but if we stand a few yards back all we can see is a blurred image, with a signature scrawled boldly across the corner.

Yet the exhibitionism and self-display and dandyish conceits have been symptoms of a necessary bravado. Whatever comes out of all this restless activity of the late fifties and early sixties, in the way of durable reputations and positive advances, we are still in the middle of a whole series of uncommonly difficult transitions, as the minority film-makers move in to fill part of the gap left by the decline of the big production empires. If iconoclasm and a certain optimistic anarchy were necessary three or four years ago, a period of consolidation and sorting out now looks equally important. Can the new film-makers take enough of the audience with them? Are we likely to have, by 1970 or so, a cinema split between the mass-entertainment movies, made at huge cost for huge audiences, and the small-scale films which have left the majority audience lagging behind? It has happened in the novel, in painting, in music, and it is not inconceivable that it could happen in the cinema. Certainly one could no more expect a mass public to go every step of the way with Antonioni or Resnais or Godard, or even Truffaut despite his sensitivity to audience response, than one could have asked them to go along with Proust or Henry James or Virginia Woolf.

If the cinema had held itself down, at any given moment, to the kind of subtleties and complexities it assumed people would be able unquestioningly to follow, we would still be back with *The Great Train Robbery* and *Rescued by Rover*. But a creative cinema which leaves too much of its audience too far behind would be running a clear risk of widening the gap, already quite wide enough, between one kind of audience and another. A snobbery of the specialized cinemas can be much more debilitating and depressing than the free-for-all in which each film takes its chance with the rest. The artist who wants to put his own vision into his work is never likely to find the going entirely smooth: imagine even a Picasso who had to beg £100,000 or so before he could put paint to canvas. And the cinema enthusiasts will always be on the side of such an artist; they will look also to the takers of chances who help to keep this immensely difficult medium alive. But the showmen who found the sun shining in Los Angeles and settled down there half a century ago to make the movies were not thinking like this. They wanted the biggest audience in the world, and they got it; and along with the audience they built an art form not quite like any other.

> The impulse which leads me to a Humphrey Bogart movie has little in common with the impulse which leads me to the novels of Henry James or the poetry of T. S. Eliot [wrote the American critic Robert Warshow]. That there is a connexion between the two impulses I do not doubt, but the connexion is not adequately summed up in the statement that the Bogart movie and the Eliot poem are both forms of art.

The new film-makers may be taking us that much closer to the James novel or the Eliot poem; but no one concerned about the future of the cinema, much less its past, would jettison the Bogart movie in the process. If the cinema ever goes out of business as a mass entertainment, then the fact that certain areas of experiment still remain open would be small consolation for anyone. We need the lot: films and movies, James and Bogart, minority art and mass medium. In spite of all the hazards of the last decade, which have produced so many dismal forecasts, so many pronouncements of commercial decline, it seems tolerably certain that the cinema will continue to give them to us. During the worst of its troubles, Hollywood adopted the defiant and appealing slogan 'Movies are better than ever'. Oddly enough, in the long run and on a world view, the publicists may have got it about right.

19 From: Film Quarterly, Vol. XVIII No. 1, Fall 1964 by Michael Roemer

THE SURFACES OF REALITY

As Siegfried Kracauer effectively demonstrates, the camera photographs the skin; it cannot function like an X-ray machine and show us what is underneath. This does not mean, however, that the film-maker has no control over the surfaces rendered by his camera. On the contrary, he *chooses* his surfaces for their content, and through their careful selection and juxtaposition builds a structure of feeling and meaning that are the core of his work.

There are times in the history of the medium when story, treatment and performance drift so far into a studio never-never land that we cannot help but make a virtue of 'pure' reality, as free from interference on the part of the film-maker as possible—even at the risk of creating something shapeless. This should not, however, obscure the fact that a film, like a poem or painting, is basically an artifact.

The assertion that film is nothing more than a documentary recording of reality undoubtedly stems from the fact that the medium must render all meaning in physical terms. This affinity for real surfaces, combined with great freedom of movement both in time and space, brings film closer than any other medium to our own random experience of life. Even the realistic playwright, who—until the advent of the camera—came closest to rendering the appearance of reality, is often forced in his structure to violate the very sense of life he is trying to create. But the film-maker can use the flexible resources at his command to approximate the actual fabric of reality. Moreover, he need not heighten his effects in order to communicate, for he can call on the same sensibilities in his audience that we use in life itself.

All of us bring to every situation, whether it be a business meeting or a love affair, a social and psychological awareness which helps us understand complex motivations and relationships.

159

This kind of perception, much of it nonverbal and based on apparently insignificant clues, is not limited to the educated or gifted. We all depend on it for our understanding of other people and have become extremely proficient in the interpretation of subtle signs—a shading in the voice, an averted glance. This nuanced awareness, however, is not easily called upon by the arts, for it is predicated upon a far more immediate and total experience than can be provided by literature and the theatre, with their dependence on the word, or by the visual arts—with their dependence on the image. Only film renders experience with enough immediacy and totality to call into play the perceptual processes we employ in life itself.

The fact that film exercises this sort of perceptual capacity is, I believe, one of its chief appeals to us. It gives us practice in the delicate and always somewhat uncertain skill of finding out what is going on. As an extreme example, take these lines from *Marty*. They are spoken in a dance hall during the first encounter between a lonely man and a lonely girl. She says: 'I'm twenty-nine years old. How old are you?' And he answers: 'Thirty-six.'

On the stage or the printed page these lines would fall ludicrously flat. But on the screen, when spoken by performers who can make every detail yield a wealth of meaning, they instantly convey—as they would in life itself—a complex web of feeling: the girl's fear that she might be too old or the man, her need to come right to the point, her relief when he turns out to be older, and finally a mutual delight that their relationship has crossed its first hurdle.

Film thrives on this kind of intimate detail, for the camera reports it so closely that nothing essential is lost to the eye or ear. The camera makes it possible to use the stuff of life itself, without amplification or overstatement and without any loss in dramatic value. What is achieved in a large action or an explicit moment on the stage can be rendered just as dramatically on the screen in small and *implicit* terms, for it is not the magnitude of a gesture that makes it dramatic but its meaning and intention.

This is *not* to say that the medium is most aptly used on the kind of everyday story told in *Marty*, or that low-key dialogue without conflict or strong feeling is always effective on the screen. I quote the scene merely as an example of the medium's capacity for finding meaning in the detail of everyday life and would like to suggest that out of such detail, out of the ordinary surfaces of life, the film-maker can structure *any* kind of situation and story—lyrical or dramatic, historical or contemporary.

Like so many films that deal with the past, Dreyer's *Passion de Jeanne d'Arc* might well have been filled with violent action and theatrical confrontations. Instead the story is told in terms of mundane detail. Thus Jeanne is betrayed at a critical moment by a priest who averts his eyes when she turns to him for help. There is no call for anything more explicit. The betrayal is what matters, and the camera renders it far more credibly and forcefully in a mundane detail than it would be in a highly dramatized gesture.

In *Rashomon* and *The Seven Samurai* Kurosawa deals with events of the thirteenth and sixteenth centuries in the most everyday terms. He knows that our basic daily experience of reality has not changed much over the centuries: a war between bandits and samurai in a feudal Japanese village was as full of mud and rain, as gritty and as grotesque as a twentieth-century skirmish. Film at its best uses the language of ordinary experience—but uses it subtly and artfully.

In a contemporary setting, Bresson's *A Man Escaped* chronicles the efforts of a French resistance fighter to break out of a German prison. Much of the film takes place within the confines of a cell, and the camera records how he painstakingly prepares his escape by fashioning tools out of spoons and rope out of blankets. It is all very ordinary and physical, but out of the grimy detail emerges a devout and heroic assertion of life and human freedom and of the need to preserve them in the face of all odds. In the hands of a sensitive film-maker the ordinary moment becomes a channel for deep feeling and a sequence of apparently insignificant scenes is structured into a world of great complexity.

This use of ordinary surfaces requires great skill and discipline since the audience can sense every false move and movement, every false note in the dialogue, every unsubstantiated relationship. The very thing that works *for* the film-maker if he can master it—reality—can quickly turn against him, so that the most ordinary moment becomes utterly unreal. Not surprisingly most directors avoid the challenge and set their stories in unfamiliar parts, among unusual people and in unusual circumstances.

Because most good films use the language of the commonplace, they tend to have an unassuming appearance, whereas films that make a large claim—that speak nobly and poetically about life, love and death—almost invariably prove to be hollow. A good film is concrete; it creates a sequence of objective situations, actual relationships between people, between people and their circumstances. Thus each moment becomes an objective correlative

161

that is, feeling (or meaning) rendered in actual, physical terms: objectified.

By contrast, most movies are a series of conventional communicative gestures, dialogues, and actions. Most movie-makers *play* on the feelings of their audience by setting up a sequence of incidents that have a proven effect. The events are not rendered; they are merely *cited*. The films do not use the vocabulary of actuality but rather a second-hand language that has proven effective in other films—a language that is changed only when the audience no longer responds.

This language of conventions gives most pictures the appearance of ludicrous unreality fifteen or twenty years after they have been acclaimed as masterpieces. The dramatic conventions of the 1940s are recognized as a system of hollow clichés by the sixties. When *The Best Years of Our Lives* was first shown, references to the war were enough to make an audience feel strongly about a situation or character without any substantiation whatever; there were feelings abroad which, when touched, produced the desired effect. By 1964 this is no longer true and the tissue of the film disintegrates.

Audiences can be 'played' by a skilful movie-maker with a fair amount of predictability, so that even discriminating audiences are easily taken in. At the beginning of Bergman's *Wild Strawberries* Professor Borg dreams that he is on a deserted street with all its doors and windows shuttered tight. He looks up at a clock that has no hands and pulls out his own watch only to find that its hands are missing also. A man appears on the corner with his head averted; when he turns, he has no face and his body dissolves into a pool on the side-walk. A glass hearse comes down the street and spills a coffin that opens. Borg approaches and discovers his own body in the coffin. The corpse comes to life and tries to pull him in.

The nightmare quality in this sequence is derivative. The deserted, shuttered street, the clock and watch without hands, the glass hearse, the faceless man are all conventions familiar to surrealist painting and literature. Bergman uses them skilfully and with conviction to produce an effect in the audience, but they are not true film images, derived from life and rendered in concrete, physical terms.

There is a similar nightmare in Dreyer's *Vampire*. A young man dreams that he has entered a room with an open coffin in it. He approaches and discovers that he himself is the corpse. The camera now assumes the point-of-view of the dead man: we look

162

up at the ceiling. Voices approach and two carpenters appear in our field of vision. They close the coffin with a lid but we continue to look out through a small glass window. Talking indistinctly, they nail down the lid and plane the edges of the wood. The shavings fall onto the window. One of them has put a candle down on the glass and wax drips onto it. Then the coffin is lifted up and we pass close under the ceiling, through a doorway, beneath the sunlit roofs and the church steeple of a small town—out into the open sky.

Here the detail is concrete: an experience is rendered, not cited; the situation is objective and out of it emerges, very powerfully, the feeling that Dreyer is after: a farewell to life, a last confined look at the earth before the coffin is lowered into the grave. Once again we note that the unassuming detail can render a complex feeling (or meaning) which eludes the more obviously ambitious but abstract statement.

Good film dialogue, too, has this concrete quality. Like the speech of everyday life, it does not tell you *directly* what is felt or meant. One might call it symptomatic dialogue: symptomatic because it is a surface manifestation of what is going on inside the person. The dialogue in most films is, of course, the opposite: a direct statement of feeling or meaning: 'I love you'; 'I am so happy'; 'You are this'; 'I am that'. But just as the action should be a physical or surface correlative that permits the audience to discover for itself the implicit meaning, so the dialogue should be a *surface* that renders its content by implication—not directly. The two lines quoted from *Marty* are good film dialogue. In contrast, here is an incident from Bergman's *The Seventh Seal*.

Shortly before his death the knight Antonius Block shares a meal with a young couple in front of their covered wagon. 'I shall always remembered this moment,' he says. 'The silence, the twilight, the bowls of strawberries and milk, your faces in the evening light. Mikhael sleeping, Jof with his lyre. I'll try to remember what we have talked about. I'll carry this moment between my hands as carefully as if it were a bowl filled to the brim with fresh milk. And it will be an adequate sign—it will be enough for me.'

Without this lengthy and explicit verbalization, one would have little insight into the feelings of Antonius Block. The situation itself does not communicate them and Bergman uses dialogue as a way of getting us to understand and feel something the film itself does not render. In Kurosawa's *Ikiru*, a petty official who is dying of cancer and trying desperately to give meaning to his life by pushing a playground project through the sterile bureaucracy, stops on his way home from work to look at the evening sky. 'It's beautiful,' he says to his companion, 'but I have no time.' Here the dialogue is part of the objective situation. No direct statement is needed since the man and his feelings are clear.

What is true for dialogue is equally true for performance. A good film performance is a carefully integrated sequence of concrete actions and reactions that render the feelings and thoughts of a character. It is not a system of hollow gestures that, like bad dialogue, *tell* the audience what is going on. Most film performances are drawn from the vast repertory of acting conventions. Conversely, the good film actor—whether trained in the Method or not—tries to render feelings through the use of surface correlatives. He is not concerned with the demonstration of feeling but with the symptom of feeling.

Chaplin's best work is continuously physical and concrete. If his performance in *The Gold Rush* had been generalized (or conventionalized) the scene in which he boils and eats his shoe would have become preposterous. He executes it, however, in the most careful physical detail. While the shoe is cooking, he pours water over it as if he were basting a bird. He carves and serves it with meticulous care, separating the uppers from the sole as though boning a fish. Then he winds the limp laces around his fork like spaghetti and sucks each nail as if it were a delicate chicken bone. Thus a totally incongruous moment is given an absolute, detailed physicality; the extraordinary is made ordinary, credible—and therefore funny.

It must be noted again that while the screen exceeds all other media in verisimilitude, its reality is nevertheless a *mode*. We appear to be looking at reality but are actually looking at a representation of it that may be as carefully structured as a still-life by Cézanne. The film-maker uses the surfaces of life itself—literal photographic images and accurately reproduced sounds. But the arrangement of these images and sounds is totally controlled. Each moment, each detail is carefully co-ordinated into the structure of the whole—just like the details in a painting or poem. By artfully controlling his images, the film-maker presents an unbroken realistic surface; he preserves the appearance of reality.

This means that he should at no time interpose himself between audience and action. He must be absent from the scene. An example of this is the use of the camera. In the standard film the

164

camera is often editorial; the director uses it to *point out* to the audience what he wants them to see. Imagine a scene between husband and wife: we see them in a medium-shot, talking; then we cut to a close-up of the woman's hand and discover that she is slipping her wedding ring off and on. The director has made his point: we now know that she is unhappily married. But by artificially lifting the detail out of context and bringing it to our attention, the autonomous reality of the scene is violated and the audience becomes aware of the film-maker. Of course a good director may also be said to use the camera editorially—to point out what he wants us to see. But he never seems to be doing so; he preserves the appearance of an autonomous reality on the screen. The moment with the ring would have been incidental to the scene—for the camera must follow the action, not lead it.

Since the process of editing is an obvious and continued intrusion by the film-maker on the material, an editor tries to make most of his cuts in such a way that the cut itself will be obscured. In order to cut from a medium-shot to a close-up of a man, he will probably use a moment when the man rises from a chair or turns rapidly. At such a time the audience is watching the action and is unaware of the jump; once again, the effort is to preserve an apparently autonomous reality.

At the end of *Notti di Cabiria* the girl and the man she has just married are sitting in a restaurant. We see her from the back, talking. Then Fellini cuts to a shot from the front and we see that she has taken out a large wad of bank notes—her savings. We immediately realize, with something of a shock, that the man is after her money. If Fellini had actually *shown* us Cabiria taking the money out of her pocketbook, the moment would have become self-conscious and overloaded with meaning; we would have had too much time to get the point. By jumping the moment and confronting us suddenly with the money, Fellini renders the meaning *and* preserves the apparent autonomy of the situation.

Spontaneity, the sense that what is happening on the screen is happening for the first time and without plan or direction, is an essential factor in establishing a reality. It is also extremely difficult to achieve, since a huge industry has sprung up around the medium, putting enormous financial and technical pressure on the moment before the camera. Years of routine and a high degree of established skill in every department of film-making all conspire against it. From writing and casting to the angles of the camera a monstrous if unintended predictability crushes

165

all life. Even a strong director is often helpless against the machinery; and even location shooting, which should be a liberating force, turns into a dead-end when a huge crew descends on the place, seals it off hermetically and effectively turns it into a studio. The channels have been set up too long and too well; all vision is trapped into standardized imagery and the living moment cannot survive.

For this reason an almost improvised film—like *Shadows* or *Breathless*, made without great skill or art by relatively inexperienced people—can carry far greater conviction than the standard theatrical product. In spite of obvious flaws there is a spontaneity to the action that endows it with life. Of course the experienced director, working in freedom and under good conditions, can achieve spontaneity without relying on improvisation. Kurosawa shot parts of *The Seven Samurai* with several cameras; this made it unnecessary for the actors to repeat, and so deaden, the action with every shift in camera position. Chaplin, on the other hand, used to rehearse and shoot endlessly to achieve a perfect but seemingly effortless result. Both men were after the same thing: spontaneity—and with it, reality.

Our sense of reality is so delicately attuned that certain moments are better left off the screen or the situation is destroyed. This is especially true for violence and death. When someone's head is cut off in a fiction film we know perfectly well that a trick is employed and unless a scene of this kind is handled with great care, it ends up being incredible or even funny. Similarly, when someone dies on the screen and remains in full view, many of us cannot resist watching for the slightest sign of life in the supposed corpse. We are putting our own sense of reality against the movie-maker's; needless to say, *we* come out on top and the scene is destroyed.

In Dreyer's unproduced script on the life of Christ he describes the crucifixion by showing us the back of the cross, with the points of the nails splintering through the wood. On the screen those would be undeniably real nails going through real wood, and the authenticity of the moment would not be challenged. If, however, Dreyer had chosen to show us the cross from the front we would know absolutely that the nails going through the *flesh* are a deception—and the suffering figures would turn into a performer.

The nail splintering through the wood forces us to use our imagination—forces us to visualize what is happening on the other side of the cross. This involves us in a far deeper participation than could be achieved by the spurious horror of a nail going through the flesh of an actor.

There is something to be learned here about the entire process of perception in film. If we are explicitly told something, as we are in most pictures, we remain passive and essentially outsiders. If, however, we have to draw our *own* conclusions on the basis of evidence presented, as we do in life itself, we cannot help but participate. We become actively involved. When we are told something explicitly, we are in a sense deprived of the experience. It has been digested for us and we are merely informed of the results, or the meaning. But it is *experience* we are after, even if it remains vicarious experience.

This brings us to another characteristic of the medium—one that is profoundly related to our previous discussion. Although the experience of the motion-picture audience remains essentially vicarious, film comes closer than any other medium to giving us the illusion of a *primary* experience. This has been studied by psychologists who have found that the dark theatre, the bright hypnotic screen, the continuous flow of images and sounds, and the large anonymous audience in which we are submerged all contribute to a suspension of self-awareness and a total immersion in the events on the screen.

Beyond this, however, the medium itself encourages the illusion of a primary participation. The camera can induce an almost physical response—so that when Chaplin sits on a hypodermic needle in the lair of a dope fiend, or when Dreyer's Jeanne d'Arc has her head shaved and some of the hair falls onto her lip, the sensation produced in us is almost physical. Moreover, this physical participation is not limited to sharp sensory detail; it extends to the realm of movement.

Most directors think of the screen as of a *picture frame* within which each shot is carefully composed. They emphasize the *pictorial* quality of film. But while the medium is visual, it is not pictorial in the conventional sense. A sequence of beautifully composed shots tends to leave the audience outside the frame— spectators who are continually aware of the director's fine eye for composition. A good director tries to eliminate this distance between audience and action, to destroy the screen as a picture frame, and to drag the audience *through* it into the reality of the scene. That is the function of the running shots in *Rashomon* and of the extraordinarily emphatic camerawork of Fellini, who leans subtly into every movement and propels us into the action kinesthetically. By contrast, we have the autonomous camera motion and stiff pictorial composition of most films.

Images of movement rather than beautifully composed shots are at the heart of the medium, and significantly some of the most haunting moments in film derive their effect from motion. In Vigo's *L'Atalante*, a bride on her wedding night, still dressed in her white gown, walks along the deck of a moving barge. The barge moves forward, she is walking toward the stern, and the camera is set on the edge of the canal, so that there is a dark stationary line in the foreground. The combination of the silent forward gliding of the barge, with the backward motion of the girl, whose gown and veil are streaming in the wind, has a profound emotional impact; it renders perfectly both her feelings and our own.

At the end of *Ikiru* the dying bureaucrat has succeeded in building the playground. It is a winter night; the camera moves slowly past a jungle-gym; beyond it we see the old man, swaying to and fro on a child's swing and singing to himself under the falling snow. The various components of this scene are hard to separate: the hoarse, cracked voice of the dying man; his happiness; the song itself. But the motion of the camera, the falling snow, and the slow movement of the swing certainly contribute to the extraordinary sense of peace and reconciliation that is communicated by the image.

A last example: in Dreyer's *Day of Wrath* a witch is burned in a seventeenth-century town. We see her bound to the top rungs of a tall ladder. Then Dreyer cuts to a long-shot and side view: on the left a huge pile of faggots is burning; to the right soldiers are raising the ladder toward the fire by means of long poles. When it stands perpendicular, they topple it forward so that the woman falls screaming across the entire frame toward the flames. The falling arc described by the victim is rendered in coldly objective terms, from far away—but it transmits her terror completely and draws us relentlessly into the action.

Kurosawa has developed a way of stating that makes it hard for an audience to remain detached. On the theory that no one should be seen entirely from the back, many directors stage their scenes in a three-quarter view. As a result, no one is seen full-face: *we* look at the actors, but they look away. In *Rashomon* and *The Seven Samurai*, however, the actors either have their backs to camera or face us frontally. When they face us, they are all but looking at us—with only their eyes turned slightly left or right of lens to indicate that they are addressing each other and not us. Of

168

course, a face seen frontally is much more exposed than a three-quarter view, and far less likely to leave us detached.

Film can further strengthen the illusion of a primary experience by using a subjective point-of-view. In the ancient and Elizabethan theatres, while we remain in objective possession of the entire stage, the poetry and particularly the soliloquy can focus our attention on one person and shift it to his point-of-view. At any given moment the world can be seen through his eyes, subjectively. In the realistic theatre, with its fidelity to the surfaces of everyday life, this has become difficult if not impossible. We *know* how Ibsen's Nora sees the world but except for rare moments do not *experience* it from her point-of-view. She cannot, as it were, reach out and envelop us in her vision—as Hamlet and Lear can.

On the screen it again becomes possible to shift from an objective vision of a person to a vision of what *he* sees. This is done continually, often with little understanding or control. We see a girl enter a room in an objective shot. Then the camera renders what *she* sees: there is a party and her husband is talking to another woman. The next moment might be objective again, or it might be seen from the husband's point-of-view. Montage makes it possible to shift from objective to subjective, or from one subjective point-of-view to another. Film can render a place, a person, or a situation not just as they are but in the context of the protagonist's experience—*as* his experience. A point-of-view can be so carefully articulated that we comprehend every object, every passing figure, every gesture and mood in terms of the protagonist. The medium thus extends the meaning of realistic surfaces beyond their objective value; it renders them in their subjective context as well.

This brings us to an apparent paradox, for we have insisted throughout that film is at its best when rendering an objective situation. It is true, of course, that a moment can be rendered subjectively on the screen and still retain its objective reality. When the girl sees her husband talking to another woman, we see them through her eyes and so become privy to a subjective state. But the husband and the other woman are *in themselves* rendered objectively: they look no different; they are not affected by the point-of-view. The basic language of the medium, the realistic surface, has not been violated. The same may be said of most flash-backs: a subjective recollection is rendered—but in objective, undistorted terms.

There are, however, moments on the screen in which the realistic surface is in fact destroyed and a purely subjective state is created. The processional at the end of Vigo's *Zero de Conduite* is shot in slow-motion, with the boys in their white gowns gliding through a snow of pillow feathers to the accompaniment of a totally distorted but oddly ecstatic song. In such scenes, and it must be noted that while they are often attempted they do not often succeed, the reality of the feeling is so compelling that an audience accepts and assimilates a totally subjective image. The participation is so intensive that instead of rejecting an image we know to be 'unreal', we enter into it eagerly.

When successful, scenes, of this kind are deeply moving for they are predicated on a rare and free flow of feeling between audience and material. But they are moments of grace and cannot be counted on—like those rare moments in a performance when pure feeling breaks out of the actor and is communicated directly, without the mediation of a physical correlative.

By and large the language of the medium remains the surface of reality, and there seem to be few experiences that cannot be rendered in this language. Moreover, there is a great challenge in making the commonplaces of life, that have so long eluded art, yield up their meaning and take their rightful place in the larger patterns of existence. Film is indeed, as Kracauer put it, the redemption of physical reality. For we are finally able to use the much-despised and ephemeral detail of everyday life, the common physical dross, and work it into the gold of art.

Select Further Reading

GENERAL

Boorstin, D. *The Image*, Penguin, 1963

Brown, J. A. C. *The Techniques of Persuasion*, Penguin, 1963

Cherry, C. 'World Communication' 3 Cantor lectures, printed in
  The Journal of the Royal Society of Arts, 1966

The Granada Lectures

Thompson, D. (ed.) *Discrimination and Popular Culture*, Penguin,
  1964

Williams, R. *Communications*, Chatto & Windus, 1966

THE PRESS AND ADVERTISING

The Economist Intelligence Unit. *The National Newspaper Industry*,
  1966

Ingman, D. *Television Advertising*, Business Publications, 1965

Ogilvy, D. *Confessions of an Advertising Man*, Longmans, 1964

Turner, E. S. *The Shocking History of Advertising*, Penguin, 1965

Williams, F. *The Right to Know: The Rise of the World Press*,
  Longmans, 1969

BROADCASTING

Briggs, A. *History of Broadcasting in the United Kingdom*. Vol. 1:
  The Birth of Broadcasting, Oxford University Press, 1961. Vol. 2:
  The Golden Age of Wireless, Oxford University Press, 1965

Educational Television and Radio in Britain, BBC, 1966

Friendly, F. *Due to Circumstances beyond our Control*, MacGibbon and Kee, 1967

Halloran, J. D. *The Effects of Mass Communication* (Working paper no. 1 of the Television Research Committee), Leicester University Press, 1964

Attitude Formation and Change (Working paper no. 2 of the Television Research Committee), Leicester University Press, 1967

Hood, S. *A Survey of Television*, Heinemann, 1967

Schramm, Wilbur, Jack Lyle, and Edwin B. Parker. *Television in the Lives of our Children*, Oxford University Press, 1961

Television Research Committee. *Second Progress Report and Recommendations*, Leicester University Press, 1969

FILM

Durgnat, R. *Films and Feelings*, Faber, 1967

Eisenstein, S. *Notes of a Film Director*, Lawrence & Wishart, 1959

Kitses, J. and Mercer A., *Talking about the Cinema*, British Film Institute, 1966

Stephenson, R. and Debrix, J. *The Cinema as Art*, Penguin, 1965